There is Still Time…

Francis T. Green

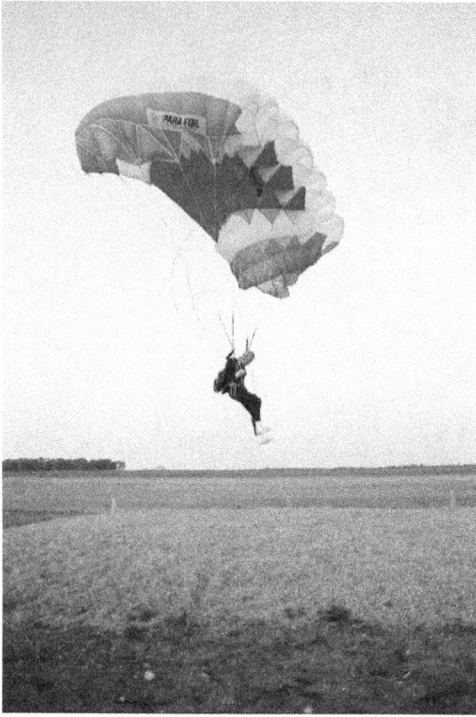

Ron Green at his best

To my wife, Tammy, and sons Zeke and Silas treasured and loved gifts from God.

Thank you to Kevin Kelle and also the entire Band of Brothers at Holy Cross Lutheran Church for teaching me so much of what is written here. All men need a Band of Brothers, *As iron sharpens iron, so one man sharpens another. Proverbs 27:17*

TABLE OF CONTENTS

I resonate with these words from the Scriptures written by the Apostle Paul. It is truly how I feel as I approached the task of writing this book:

And I came to you in weakness and in fear and in much trembling. My speech and my proclamation were not with plausible words of wisdom, but with a demonstration of the Spirit and of power, so that your faith might rest not on human wisdom but on the power of God. (1 Corinthians 2:3-5 New Revised Standard Version)

This book is the result of much "encouragement" from my family and I hope prodding of the Holy Spirit. I have experienced a growing concern over the decline of the church and the rise of Atheism in our culture. The book is certainly not an exhaustive defense of Christianity and argument against Atheism. Rather, it is meant to facilitate a journey of discovery. I hope that there is enough written on the debate between Christianity and Atheism to engage the reader to continue in the book spending some time considering the Bible. The Bible is all about Jesus and I believe that if one simply pauses long enough to look at who Jesus is; one will discover the Truth. If one is willing to approach Jesus with an open mind, He will reveal Himself and show you the very thing you are looking for.

Blessings,

Fran Green

PART ONE

Let's embark on an adventure to find what you're looking for!!!

1

I Still Haven't Found What I'm Looking For

- U2, The Joshua Tree

Beginning our Search!

Date of accident: June 18, 1996.

Location : Cedar Valley Parachute Center, Cedar Valley Airport, Utah

Deceased: Tandem Examiner: Ronald Green, age 54.

Tandem Examiner for Strong Enterprises. Over 30 years in the sport, with over 13,000 skydives including approximately 4,000 tandem jumps.

Deceased: Tandem Instructor Candidate: XXXXXXXX, age 30,

765 jumps. This was her third jump in the Tandem Certification Course.

Equipment: Dual Hawk Tandem System owned by Cedar Valley Parachute Center. All major components were found to be standard equipment manufactured by Strong Enterprises and were found to be in airworthy condition.

SYNOPSIS

=========

An emergency situation developed when the drogue bridle became half hitched around the crown of the drogue upon activation. It appears the reserve ripcord was pulled before the Candidate identified the problem. This allowed the reserve pilot chute to entangle with the drogue canopy. The reserve bridle wrapped around the lower drogue bridle before the drogue had been released. The main cutaway handle had not been activated, nor had the Examiner Safety cutaway handle been pulled. The passenger main release handle had been activated and the Examiner Safety reserve handle had been activated. The drogue and portions of both reserve and main canopies were out in the airstream and non-functional.

JUMP ANALYSIS

===============

The pair was performing their third tandem parachute jump during a Tandem Instructor Certification Course. All indications show that all equipment was in place and functional. The jump altitude was 9,000 feet AGL, from a

Cessna 182 aircraft. The pilot observed the pair exit in a stable position, then shut the door. It appears the Candidate initially pulled the drogue bridle instead of the drogue pud. Next either the Candidate or the Examiner pulled the drogue through the loose bridle resulting in the bridle knotting around the top of the drogue. This inverted the drogue within four feet of the drogue release location, rendering it useless.

It appears the reserve ripcord was then activated by the Candidate, with the reserve pilot chute lodging in the inverted drogue. The reserve bridle wrapped 11 times around the four feet of exposed drogue bridle. The student/passenger main release handle was pulled, but because of no drag on the drogue, the main did not freely extract from the container. It is believed the Examiner and Candidate tried to jar the main bag loose and manually deploy the lines. The reserve canopy was observed to be partially loose and visible but not able to inflate because a portion of the drogue bridle and the empty main bag had wrapped around the lines below the slider.

The Examiner Safety Handle on the reserve side had been activated and was found approximately 75 yards from the impact site. The reserve ripcord was not recovered, nor were the reserve closing loops.

The Cypres had activated but there were no signs of closing loop fibers in the cutters, indicating that the reserve had been activated by hand at an altitude above 2,000 ft. AGL.

The tandem pair impacted with the reserve canopy and some of the main canopy exposed. The impact site was approximately one mile from the drop zone in an open field.[1]

An exciting way to begin a book? Perhaps it grabbed your attention. Maybe it's somewhat difficult to understand, and you may have skipped right over it finding yourself right here searching for the beginning of the book. That's okay; we can begin here. The previous pages are a fatality report and an investigation into a skydiving accident. I suppose I've been thinking a lot about this accident lately, which occurred so long ago because I am the same age when Ron Green, my second cousin and one of those killed in the accident, died. He was 54. Also, there have been many in my church, family, and friends that have died recently, which has caused me to think about all of this, life and such, perhaps with a new or renewed sense of urgency.

I have read this report so many times and have studied it trying to put myself in the situation in hopes of understanding it better. Although I have not experienced the exact circumstances, I have thousands of jumps including tandem master/instructor and also acting as the passenger during tandem training jumps.

The instructor candidate made a mistake within a few seconds of exiting the aircraft. Next, a series of procedures took place, which left the pair freefalling at speeds approaching 180 miles per hour with a reserve and main parachute tangled mess trailing behind them only a few feet above their backs. Attempts were undoubtedly made to manually pull whatever canopy and material they could grab out into the air. This mess would slow their rate of fall. However, it would not be enough to save their lives.

Whenever I sit and ponder this accident, I cannot help but see Ron frantically trying to clear the mess. He had over 13,000 jumps with much experience in emergency situations, with students, as well as malfunctioning parachutes. He knew exactly what was going on; I have no doubt. The "last resort" for emergency procedures in skydiving is to pull and pound on the container, and whatever fabric is within reach in hopes of the airstream pulling out the rest to initiate inflation of the material. Indicators show that one or both of the jumpers had attempted manual deployment. Ron knew his fate! You might be asking why am I spending so much time analyzing? That's a great question, and I believe one that will be answered as we proceed.

One of the specific things that I have thought about on this accident is in trying to determine when Ron knew his fate. I estimate that the entire incident took at most 50 seconds. The early portion of the jump and the sequence of events up until manually wrestling with the parachutes probably took 30 seconds.. I know that seems fast. However, you need to remember that for Ron especially, this is second nature. Under normal circumstances, a tandem master and student exit an aircraft and are in free fall with an inflated drogue parachute (this is the small parachute that slows the tandem pair of jumpers until it is released after that it pulls out the main canopy) within five seconds. So, after exiting the aircraft, Ron and the instructor candidate have a problem within five seconds immediately taking action to resolve it. Sit and watch the second hand on a clock for 30 seconds, and you will see that that is much time, especially if one is focused on a task.

Therefore, I believe Ron had approximately 20 seconds of realizing he was going to die. Troubling, isn't it? At least I think it is troubling. Again, you may be wondering what the point of dwelling on this might be. What would you do if you KNEW you had 20 seconds to live, or 30 or even one minute? Let's let that simmer for a time…

Turning 50 and moving into the sixth decade of life is often one of those times, at least for many, when we are confronted with an earnestness that our time is short; that our lives go very quickly. 'Hey, I'm not going to live forever!' 'Wow, the time has gone fast!' and any number of similar time and age-related thoughts pop into our minds. Have you ever said or thought those words? They are true, aren't they? Many questions surface, some for the first time, some with increasing intensity. What have I done with my life? Have I made a difference? Will anyone remember me when I'm gone? What happens when I die? Will I go to heaven? Is this all there is? Have you ever wondered if there is still time to live a life of impact and meaning, to find what you're looking for…at your age? Is it too late?

Our lives are an ebb and flow of "what I am looking for" and "then what?" We are prodded and driven in pursuit of something to fulfill us, something to satisfy a craving or desire, to give our lives meaning. It is a search for peace. Sometimes you can find your own "thing," yet you must keep striving because something inside will continue stirring, haunting, whispering, "I still haven't found what I'm looking for." You may find temporary fulfillment, perhaps a career, a relationship, a hobby; or seek happiness in unhealthy pursuits such as chemical addictions, an affair, or a consuming relationship with an occupation. The momentary thrill or satisfaction will soon stir the question inside, "and then what?"

This phase of life, 50 and older, - some call it the "Fall" season of life, is often a significant turning point for many. Dr. Tim Elmore lays out what are usually the stages that occur in men up to age 50:

Phases Too Many Males Experience (Tim Elmore 2014)

- **In our 20s, males often experience either DRIVE or DISTRACTION.** By this I mean, guys either become driven by a goal in their career, or they become distracted by the malaise of options in this life-stage, such as playing video games, going clubbing, exchanging partners, etc. They're entertained by their pursuit of a goal or by all the amusements that adult life affords them. Both preoccupy them.

And then what...? (My addition)

- **In our 30s, males often experience DISAPPOINTMENT.** In this life station, guys frequently feel at least slight disappointment that the life they had envisioned isn't entirely turning out as they predicted. Neither the drive nor the distractions have satisfied them. They begin to try harder or make shifts in an attempt to become the man they assumed they were.

And then what...? (My addition)

- **In our 40s, males often experience DISSATISFACTION.** In midlife, guys begin to make moves in an attempt to fill what's still empty in their lives. In the 1980s, we began to call this "mid-life crisis." The problems become an identity problem. Dissatisfied with their identity or their accomplishments, guys often seek answers in a new spouse, a new car, a new job or some new status.

And then what...? (My addition)

- **In our 50s, males often experience DISILLUSIONMENT.** In post-midlife, men have either become fulfilled with the moves they made in their 40s, or they become disillusioned. In reply, they either cover up their sadness, or they

22

become bitter, eventually evolving into the grumpy old men we all want to avoid when we meet them.[2]

And then what…?

Have you noticed men over 50 who seem to drift along in lives without drive, passion or purpose and how this often manifests itself in wasted hours in front of the television or other mindless pursuits? I imagine all of us can think of men stuck in any one of the phases above. Of course, this is not merely a problem for men over 50, but the focus of this book is on the over 50 demographic. Currently, over 100 million Americans are over the age of 50, and 70 percent of those between the ages of 50-64 are diagnosed with at least one chronic illness. Anxiety and depression are on the rise, and self-described boredom is frequently reported in this age group as well. Suicide rates are rising, "The most pronounced increases were seen among men in their 50s, a group in which suicide rates jumped by nearly 50 percent, to about 30 per 100,000" (CDC).

I recently heard a quote that captures much of the underlying problem, "Happy, but not fulfilled." That indeed says a lot, doesn't it? There is so much happiness

23

to be found or purchased, but fulfillment? That's a bit more elusive.

The "Graying of America" is happening before our eyes as the last of the baby boomers are moving into their fifties. I believe that our materialistic culture's vision for retirement is also a contributor to the problem. As this group receives their AARP applications in the mail one can't help but wonder if one has made an impact in life; is there meaning in life?[3] **Not surprisingly, some dread turning 50 along with the above-mentioned mental changes.**

Dread. The word just breeds negativity! Things look pretty bleak by now, wouldn't you say? I am hopeful that this book will guide men through a process of evaluating their lives and set them on a course of adventure, - an adventure of living fully alive in your best years!

There is Still Time will help you find exactly what you are looking for. I hope to facilitate thoughts and discussion as we think about TIME, our TIME (see T.I.M.E. #1 later in the book) and how we could spend it to find what we are looking for as we satisfy "and then what?". The point in time that you currently see yourself could be the point where you look at who you have become in your journey of life and no matter where you now find yourself, set a new course to living a life of impact, purpose, and meaning

2

God, my soul thirsts for you; my whole body longs for you.

- King David

The phone is ringing as I step out of the shower trying to grab a towel while I locate the phone quickly. "Ron Green went in" the voice on the other end stated. My mind began to replay memories and years of shared experiences with Ron. Wow. I suppose one is not surprised in hearing of a skydiving fatality and many, skydivers, in particular, said these words: "At least he died doing what he loved." I can almost hear what was certainly spoken and thought by many people, "I'm sure that if he had it to do all over again, Ron wouldn't change a thing." But, I wonder…did Ron find what he was looking for?

ANOTHER SKYDIVING STORY…

Have you ever awakened in the hospital wondering whether it was all just a bad dream or if the nightmare you "dreamt" actually happened? August 10, 1985, is the day I began an extended education in life. Granted, I did not start college or any formal programs, but that day in August drastically altered the course of my life. Little did I know that this day would have an impact that continues even today.

August 10, 1985, was a Saturday. It was a beautiful hot and sunny day in my hometown of Allison, Iowa. I arose early in the morning, hopped into my recently purchased Toyota pickup, which I had loaded the night before and raced off to Algona, - a short two hours away. I had been anticipating this day with much excitement. You know the type, right? I arrived at Algona municipal airport where I met my cousin Ron and his wife Mary, and Ron Nowak. We all loaded our equipment into Ron's Cessna 172 and flew off to Johnston, Iowa – a suburb of Des Moines. The air was a bit bumpy, and we could sense that it was going to be a pretty typical hot, windy August day in the Midwest. We landed at the small airport in Johnston and immediately jumped into a car and drove over to look at our landing area for the day's activities.

I was a member of Green's Flight and Freefall, a demonstration skydiving team owned and operated by my cousin Ron and his wife, Mary. We performed shows for small communities in the Midwest, often for annual town festivals, county fairs, etc. On this day, we were scheduled for a morning and an afternoon jump.

This day was not unlike most other days where we had performed. The morning jump went smoothly as I was the first jumper to exit the aircraft. After a short ten-second free fall, I opened my parachute and then opened a smoke canister, which painted the path of spirals and twists as I navigated to the landing area amidst the cheers of the crowd. Next, Ron Nowak, a friend of Ron and Mary's performed a similar jump, which also went off without a problem. Finally, Ron Green, the most experienced jumper in our group with more than 5,000 jumps at that time and a world-class accuracy jumper, landed precisely on a 5-inch diameter circle target to the delight of the crowd. We all packed our parachutes while people walked among us asking questions about parachuting, and then we loaded the car and returned to the airport.

The afternoon performance was to be the same routine, regarding our show. As is often the case in the Midwest in the heart of summer, afternoon heat is usually accompanied by gusty winds. This was indeed the case this day as our airplane ride to the 5,000 feet exit altitude was bumpy and rough. I exited the plane, enjoyed the cooler air as I fell for 10-15 seconds before opening my parachute. I immediately oriented myself to the landing area and opened the smoke canister for the crowd below. The parachute ride was much different than the morning jump, and I could feel the parachute struggling to make forward penetration against the strong August winds. I carefully flew the parachute to the landing area setting up for final approach at approximately 300 feet above the ground. The target was set in a grassy field with trees and power lines outlining the upwind border. The trees broke much of the wind gusts while also causing turbulence in the air for my parachute. As I began my final approach towards the target, my parachute surged and increased in forward speed as I quickly headed for the trees and power lines that lie ahead. I sensed a hazardous situation, panicked and cranked a hard right turn to steer away from the high voltage lines. This radical turn in combination with the high, gusty winds caused a "slingshot" effect of whipping me into the ground from above treetop height impacting the ground with severe force. According to witnesses, and as was reported in *USA Today,* the sound of my bones breaking could be heard from a football field distance.

I lay crumpled and broken on the ground with shattered femurs in both legs and a lacerated chin. An ambulance took me to nearby Veteran's Hospital in Des Moines. My parents arrived at the hospital a few hours later and immediately began to assess the situation. Knowing that a better-equipped hospital was nearby, they transferred me to Mercy Hospital. They put me in traction, and the orthopedist discussed surgical procedures required for treatment. Shortly after, I needed blood transfusions and began to have major complications where bone marrow and particles from within my broken femurs were entering the bloodstream presenting life-threatening complications. The medical team painted a dim picture as many times this condition is fatal. Our pastor and my family were notified to come and visit since survival was looking doubtful.

Many long days of prayer and waiting followed. Thankfully, I do not have a great deal of memory from these early days following the crash. I do remember times of extreme pain and moments of what must have been hallucinations and odd dreams most likely from the powerful pain medications that I was on. Well, you're reading what I have written, so I obviously made it through this scare.

Yes, I would live, but this was the beginning, the start of a long process of recovery, a long journey of discovery. I vividly remember these days, as they were long and painful. Internal rods, and wires to hold my bones together were inserted in both femurs. Three weeks after the accident and one day after surgery to put the rods in place, I was taken to physical therapy. Wheeling my chair in the area in front of the parallel bars, I was helped to my feet to stand. What a combination of pain and also excitement at finally being out of my hospital bed! As I looked across the room into the full-length mirror at my broken and atrophied legs, I couldn't recognize the skinny and broken person who looked back at me. I held myself upright with my arms preparing to walk again. I had no idea the long, arduous road that lies ahead.

Though I would never wish a situation like this on anyone, the education gained through the experience cannot be learned in a classroom. The lessons taught me perseverance, sacrifice, discipline, and leadership to name but a few. Most importantly, I learned to be grateful! I now consider the accident a blessing.

I am sure you have read or heard of other "near death" experiences. Perhaps you've had your own, but to say that they are life changing is an understatement and truly a cliché. I believe they are a gift from God. As it is when something is taken away, you realize what you had. Up until this point in my life, I lived completely for my enjoyment and me. Laying in a hospital bed, totally dependent on others even to go to the bathroom forces some serious introspection. "And then what?" What is the point of this thing called life? Why am I here and what is my role in all of this?

"My child, don't ignore it when the Lord disciplines you and don't be discouraged when he corrects you. For the Lord disciplines those he loves, and he punishes those he accepts as his children." (Hebrews 12:5-6 NIV)

Purpose and Meaning
When I think about my life and the place where I find myself, I see God's leading and working. It is interesting how God has used two skydiving accidents for His glory

and purpose (my opinion of course). These two events have propelled and given me fuel to live for Him. I desire to share Jesus with any who will listen. It is my conviction and belief that Jesus and a relationship with Him, are what everyone is ultimately looking for, whether we know or believe that or not. Jesus is the foundation upon which, - meaning, purpose, and a life of fulfillment is built. I hope that you will take the time to think deeply about life – your life. Have you found what you're looking for? There is a life to come, and this life is to be lived in preparation for that life. I hope you will journey with me.

Who am I?
"Don't you fear God," he said, "since you are under the same sentence?" (Luke 23:40 NIV)
"Do not be afraid of those who kill the body but cannot kill the soul. Rather, be afraid of the One who can destroy both soul and body in hell." (Matthew 10:28 NIV)

After we learned of Ron's death, we received word that there wasn't going to be a Christian funeral just a celebration, a wake in his hometown of Thompson, Iowa, at the local bar *The Branding Iron*. Of course, it would be a celebration – Skydive-Style, including a keg(s) of beer and great stories of life in skydiving. His ashes were later scattered over Skydive Arizona. I could not make it to either event (admittedly, in hindsight, I had no desire to be a part of them), but my Grandma Green attended the wake. She filled me in on the details later and was quite upset about the whole event. She said that she decided to approach Ron's wife Mary and ask her why she did not have a funeral for Ron in church and a proper "Christian" burial. Mary informed my Grandmother that Ron never actually believed any of that God stuff and did not desire to have a Christian funeral.

My grandma asked me what I thought about it all, and I had to admit, I did not know. I did not know because Ron and I never talked about God or matters of faith; we were only having fun skydiving when we were together. Skydiving was life for both of us. As I think back to the hours we spent together, I do not remember having any spiritual conversations. I wish now that we would have; although I was living just like Ron during all of our time together. It was only after my skydiving accident and subsequent time serving in the Air Force that I began to find what I was looking for.

Often people feel the need to step in here and say something like, "So, you believe Ron is in hell, huh?" Or the desire might be to get on a tangent about how could I be so narrow-minded that I believe Jesus is the only way. Before I go any further, I do not claim to be a judge. Thankfully, I am not qualified to decide where people will be spending their eternities. Jesus Himself said that He did not come to judge the world, but to save it. I try to follow Him, knowing that I come up short. But, Jesus also said, "I am the way, the truth, and the life." I do not judge, but I believe Jesus is the only way because He said so. A life of meaning and impact must be built off a relationship with Him. Please hang with me here.

Let's talk about it now. My conviction is to call any and all who will listen to the most critical adventure they could live, and that is the adventure of living for Jesus. Ron had the same upbringing as I, probably similar to many reading this. He grew up in small-town Iowa and went to a Lutheran church. He was baptized as an infant, he went to church, Sunday school, and was confirmed during his middle school years. What happened?

I will never know Ron's core beliefs beyond knowing that we both experienced a traditional Lutheran education in the faith. The outward fruit of his life appeared clear; it was all about skydiving. He did tell me that he was finally living the dream. He wanted his entire life to be able to skydive for a living, and he was finally able to do that moving to Skydive Arizona in Eloy, AZ after years of working at Winnebago Industries in Forest City, Iowa. Apparently, he achieved his lifelong dreams...and then he died. Is that it? Did he find what he was looking for? To live a life of self-indulgence, seeking happiness each day through serving oneself? Is that the goal of life, to find the activity, job, or whatever pleasure and then we die? It is true that Ron did serve others and taught many people how to skydive. He brought many people joy through exhibition skydiving and his friendly attitude. Had he honestly found what he was looking for? I believe that meaning and purpose in life are only found in a person; Jesus Christ.

I know that Ron grew up as a Lutheran Christian. I know that he learned and had the same foundation of beliefs that many people have. What is troubling to me is that these core beliefs did not seem to manifest themselves in shaping Ron's life to live for Jesus. Where was the relationship with Jesus?

Some may argue that a life-changing, near-death experience often impacts you to think more deeply about life's brevity or to open up to matters of faith. I believe that is true in many cases. It does not appear to be the case for Ron though; of course, we cannot know the answer. He had two prior near-death experiences in his life. Both related to skydiving and both times we thought he would not survive. But, he did, and he continued to skydive and live in the same manner he always had.

Perhaps it is a church thing. The argument has been around a long time now that men hate going to church. Church is boring, it is filled with a bunch of hypocrites, and the list goes on and on. Many are or were at one time forced to go to church, and when the time came to make their own decision, the choice was to walk away from it all, church and Jesus. We will talk more about the church later.

In all of the time I spent with Ron, we simply did not discuss matters of faith. This has bothered me since Ron's death and has driven me to re-hash all the wasted opportunities. We should have talked about faith. We should have discussed the big questions of life. We should have discussed Jesus.

The Apostle Paul writes these words in Acts 20:24, "But my life is worth nothing unless I use it for doing the work assigned me by the Lord Jesus – the work of telling others the Good News about the wonderful Grace of God."

That is the focus of this book. I have shared this story and given this talk to youth and adults alike in hopes that many will be saved because of it. I pass out and keep a business card with these words on it: WHOSE PAUL AM I? And on the back is the verse quoted above, Acts 20:24. There is no more important message!!

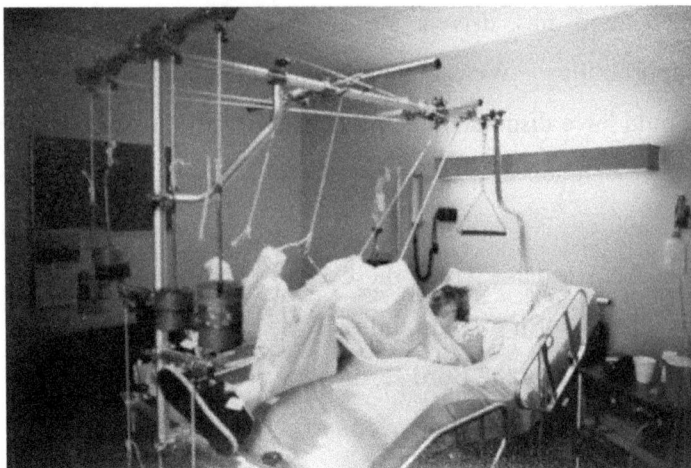

The author following the skydiving accident

3

God?

Is there a God? That is indeed a question that has been debated throughout history, and it is a question very much alive today. Maybe Ron concluded that God does not exist. Perhaps you are unsure and struggle with the thought of God. The debate in our modern times, at least in the West, is a debate between Science and Religion and most often includes evolution versus creation. It is beyond the scope of this book to discuss all of the nuances of each category; for simplicity let's consider only atheists and theists. These broad categories naturally include a wide range. For our purposes we will include agnostics, skeptics, etc. in the atheist group. Theists include all with a belief in some higher power, but we will be much more specific to speak of Christians and the exclusive claims of Jesus.

Richard Dawkins (see also T.I.M.E. #9 in this book) writes (page 187 of *The God Delusion)*:

The nineteenth century is the last time when it was possible for an educated person to admit to believing in miracles like the virgin birth without embarrassment. When pressed, many educated Christians today are too loyal to deny the virgin birth and resurrection. But it embarrasses them because their rational minds know that it is absurd, so they would much instead not be asked.[4]

It is my conviction that despite many atheists claims otherwise, the Christian faith possesses much evidence. The fact is that far too many people fall under the misperception that faith believes without any evidence. There is much evidence. So much of our knowledge and people's ability "to know" lie outside of the realm and capabilities of science. Further, the Creator God, this earth, and the universe, the Bible, archeology, as well as writings from outside of the Bible offer evidence for Jesus that is simply too overwhelming to ignore. I do not intend to offer a point-by-point debate-type discussion on atheism vs. Christianity, just a few thoughts for consideration. Christopher DiCarlo is a famous and outspoken professor at the University of Toronto and author of *How to Become a Really Good Pain in the Ass: A Critical Thinker's Guide* to *Asking the Right Questions.*[5] *DiCarlo* showed much wisdom when he stated before a debate with Dr. John Lennox, that each person could assume the other man's position and argue from there. Yes, each man DiCarlo the atheist and Lennox the Christian will know the points their opponent will take and should be able to articulate such. This is informative, and I also believe correct, that neither person will be able to change the other's mind. Each man is deeply committed to the FAITH that they hold. Make no mistake about it, they both possess faith in their beliefs. DiCarlo believes that this world is all that there is and that science can explain everything. What science is unable to explain is only because science hasn't yet discovered. The title of his book shows his position that "critical thinking" proves there is no God. Lennox has faith in Jesus and is a committed Christian.

Interestingly, Lennox is a brilliant scientist and mathematician; he does not discount science but believes there is much evidence for God yet much in our universe that science cannot explain. Professor Lennox and all theists believe that there is a Reality that is outside the material or physical world – God the Creator of it all.

That Creator God is the only one who can create faith. Through His Word, the Bible, and through the power of His Holy Spirit working in people's lives faith is created. The Bible itself says that "Faith comes through hearing the word of God." Romans 10:17. The Bible also says that people do know the truth about God through His Creation. Romans 1:19 NLT,

> "They know the truth about God because he has made it obvious to them. For ever since the world was created, people have seen the earth and sky. Through everything God made, they can clearly see his invisible qualities – his eternal power and divine nature. *So they have no excuse for not knowing God."* (emphasis mine) Powerful words to be sure!

Equally troubling words can be found for those who choose to reject God and His revelation of Creation. 2 Thessalonians 2:10-12, "They perish because they refused to love the truth and so be saved. For this reason, God sends them a powerful delusion, so that they will believe the lie and so that all will be condemned who have not believed the truth but have delighted in wickedness."

I don't know about you, but these words wake me up! God has and does make himself known; however, when people choose to reject God, He sends them a "delusion" and they will believe a lie, perhaps evolution. I find it fascinating that atheist Richard Dawkins titled one of his books, *The God Delusion.*

John Lennox writes:

> "Indeed, having debated with Richard Dawkins twice in public, discussed biblical miracles with him once on the air, and spent much time analyzing his arguments, I find myself more than ever convinced of the truth of the resurrection of Jesus, and the truth of the biblical prophecy concerning him."[6]

Human arguments are limited, as each comes to a point where faith is required. I believe the arguments and the evidence for God are a slam-dunk though when it comes to proof of God and must be considered as one ponders God.

The Holy Bible

The Bible must be taken seriously!!

I do not believe that one can discount the writings of Scripture. They are firmly rooted in history and are only validated and enriched by archeology and other historical writings. I suppose you can choose not to believe what you read in the Scriptures, but you cannot remove them from the historical time period in which they were written. The Bible is well corroborated and rooted in history. As such, they are a mountain of evidence, both deep and wide, of God acting in our world. Most importantly, they present the historical Jesus, the one who claimed to be God; the very one who walked this earth and died upon a cross. That is evidence that simply cannot be ignored. And make no mistake – it is a historical fact that even the most liberal scholar and atheists alike cannot and do not dismiss. It is simply not possible to claim Jesus never lived and walked the earth; at most you can reject his claims to being the Son of God and dismiss the miracles done while He lived among us.

Science does a beautiful job of explaining the physical world. Physics, biology, chemistry, and mathematics are wonderful disciplines, and I know that I benefit every day because of them. The problem I have and one that doesn't get talked about enough is when experts in these particular fields attempt to explain phenomena outside of their discipline.

Terry Eagleton, a professor of English literature at Manchester University, offers a scathing review of Richard Dawkins' *God Delusion* (Dawkins is currently and arguably the most famous spokesperson for atheism). Eagleton writes, "Imagine someone holding forth on biology whose only knowledge of the subject is the book of British birds, and you have a rough idea of what it feels like to read Dawkins on theology." Eagleton later describes Dawkins as theologically illiterate. When Dawkins or any other atheist tries to answer questions outside of science's ability we should not listen or take seriously anything they say.[7] As we move forward, we will be engaging in issues that science simply cannot answer. And the questions that we will be addressing are supported by a great deal of evidence.

So, we proceed from this point, considering, what I believe to be, much evidence beyond the debates of DiCarlo and Lennox.

I find it interesting that the Bible, God's revealed Word to humanity, tells us to do exactly that same thing. Leave the debate behind. Writing nearly 2,000 years ago, a man named Paul who became a follower of Jesus after persecuting and attempting to eliminate Jesus' followers, wrote these words:

The Wisdom of God

The message of the cross is foolish to those who are headed for destruction! But we who are being saved know it is the very power of God. As the Scriptures say,

> "I will destroy the wisdom of the wise
> and discard the intelligence of the intelligent."
> So where does this leave the philosophers, the scholars, and the world's brilliant debaters? God has made the wisdom of this world look foolish. Since God in his wisdom saw to it that the world

would never know him through human wisdom, he has used our foolish preaching to save those who believe. It is foolish to the Jews, who ask for signs from heaven. And it is foolish to the Greeks, who seek human wisdom. So when we preach that Christ was crucified, the Jews are offended and the Gentiles say it's all nonsense.

But to those called by God to salvation, both Jews, and Gentiles, Christ is the power of God and the wisdom of God. This foolish plan of God is wiser than the wisest of human plans, and God's weakness is stronger than the greatest of human strength.

Remember, dear brothers and sisters, that few of you were wise in the world's eyes or powerful or wealthy when God called you. Instead, God chose things the world considers foolish in order to shame those who think they are wise. And he chose things that are powerless to shame those who are powerful.

God chose things despised by the world, things counted as nothing at all, and used them to bring to nothing what the world considers important. As a result, no one can ever boast in the presence of God.

God has united you with Christ Jesus. For our benefit God made him to be wisdom itself. Christ made us right with God; he made us pure and holy, and he freed us from sin. Therefore, as the Scriptures say, "If you want to boast, boast only about the Lord." (1 Corinthians 1:18-31 NLT)

Aren't these words amazing?! God, speaking through the Apostle Paul, tells us that the debates of this world will not answer questions regarding Jesus. Only God can open people's hearts and minds to faith. I find that remarkable. Knowledge of God is beyond the debates of this world.

In the crucifixion of Jesus, we are talking about an actual event that occurred in history. This real incident involved a historical person named Jesus. Any discussions of God, Creation, and the like must begin with Jesus. In case you didn't already know it, here's **the Christian faith in a nutshell.**

Jesus died on a cross and rose from the dead in order to reconcile people to God. Most people have heard the words of John 3:16, "For God so loved the world that He gave His one and only Son, that whoever believes in Him will not perish, but have eternal life." The Bible agrees and tells us that it is "foolishness." It is impossible for us to believe, genuinely impossible to come to faith in Jesus without the help of God.

Why? Why did/do people need to be reconciled to God? The Grand Narrative that the Bible gives is that God is the Creator of all that is seen in our physical world. The creation was perfect in the beginning; God and people dwelling together in perfect relationship. God created people in His image with the power to choose. The first man and woman could live knowing God, listening to and following Him; or they could decide to pursue their desires (for a much more in-depth discussion see section on Bible later in the book). People chose to disobey God, and the perfect relationship was broken. Humanity very quickly declined, so much so that God was even sorry He created people. God was going to remove people entirely from the earth, but a man named Noah found favor with God and

God decided to cleanse the land and to renew people through Noah.

God made a covenant with Noah and then with a man named Abraham. God chose a people through whom He would restore relationship with Himself. He would bless the nations through His chosen people, Abraham and Israel. Judah and Israel continually struggled with the choice to follow God or to follow their desires. The relationship that was broken in the Garden at Creation caused all people to sin, to live contrary to the will of God. God states in Malachi, the final book of the Old Testament what is a summary of the people of God's living since the first sin, "Ever since the days of your ancestors you have turned aside from my statutes and have not kept them. Return to me, and I will return to you, says the Lord of hosts. But you say, "How shall we return?" (Malachi 3:7)

All humanity is born into sin; it is sometimes called original sin in the church. It merely means that ever since the first man and woman, Adam and Eve, chose to follow their ways instead of obeying God, all their offspring were born with this condition called sin.

God chose to save humanity from this condition that they were unable to change on their own. Romans 8:3, "So God did what the law could not do. He sent his own Son in a body like the bodies we sinners have. And in that body, God declared an end to sin's control over us by giving his Son as a sacrifice for our sins."

That is the Good News, also called the Gospel. Jesus died on a cross, and God raised Him from the dead to defeat sin, death, and the devil. Jesus continues to work through the church, by His Holy Spirit through the power of His spirit working through His Word, the Bible, and His people. This is the Grand Narrative of the Bible in summary.

Richard Dawkins loves to wax eloquent on the ridiculous nature of anyone being so simple-minded that they could believe in the resurrection of Jesus. Does Dawkins believe discounting a miracle because it goes against the laws of nature disproves it? God is the creator of nature; He can work outside of the laws that He created. Further, the Bible itself reports the disciples and others had a similar response to the news of Jesus' resurrection as that of Dawkins. Luke 24:9-11:

"When they came back from the tomb, they told all these things to the Eleven and to all the others. It was Mary Magdalene, Joanna, Mary the mother of James, and the others with them who told this to the apostles. *But they did not believe the women, because their words seemed to them like nonsense.*" (Emphasis mine)

"All these things" is the report that Jesus was not in the tomb. They were told and were reporting that He had risen from the dead. He did just as He had said; He conquered sin, death, and the devil. Jesus' disciples did NOT believe the news; it was nonsense to them. No, they had to be convinced. They were convinced over the next forty days as Jesus frequently appeared to them. He had fellowship with them; He ate with them. He gave them further instructions as to their mission after He departed to be with His Father. We will return to this later.

Romans 9:16 states, "So receiving God's promise is not up to us. We can't get it by choosing it or working hard for it. God will show mercy to anyone He chooses." And anticipating the many questions that will certainly arise, Romans 10:14-17:

But how can they call on him to save them unless they believe in him? And how can they believe in him if they have never heard about him? And how can they hear about him unless someone tells them? And how will anyone go and tell them without being sent? That is what the Scriptures mean when they say, "How beautiful are the feet of those who bring good news!" But not everyone welcomes the Good News, for Isaiah the prophet said, "Lord, who has believed our message?" Faith comes from listening to this message of good news – the Good News about Christ.

The entire Bible is about Jesus. It begins and ends with Him. Perhaps you do not believe the Bible is an accurate source. We'll talk more about the Bible later.

There is evidence for Jesus outside of the Bible. The Roman Emperor Nero was blaming Christians for burning Rome. Reporting on the fire that destroyed Rome in A. D. 64, the Roman historian Tacitus wrote (A.D. 116):

Nero fastened the guilt…on a class hated for their abominations, called Christians by the populace.

55

Christus, from whom the name had its origin, suffered the extreme penalty during the reign of Tiberius at the hands of...Pontius Pilate, and a most mischievous superstition, thus checked for the moment, again broke out not only in Judea, the first source of the evil, but even in Rome... [8]

Evidence for Jesus, His death, and the claim of His resurrection!

Another important source of evidence about Jesus and early Christianity is found in the letters of Pliny the Younger to Emperor Trajan. Pliny was the Roman governor of Bithynia in Asia Minor. In one of his letters, dated around A.D. 112, he asks Trajan's advice about the appropriate way to conduct legal proceedings against those accused of being Christians. Pliny says that he needed to consult the emperor about this issue because a great multitude of every age, class, and sex stood accused of Christianity.

At one point in his letter, Pliny relates some of the information he has learned about these Christians:

They were in the habit of meeting on a certain fixed day before it was light, when they sang in alternate verses a hymn to Christ, as to a god, and bound themselves by a solemn oath, not to any wicked deeds, but never to commit any fraud, theft or adultery, never to falsify their word, nor deny a trust when they should be called upon to deliver it up; after which it was their custom to separate, and then reassemble to partake of food – but food of an ordinary and innocent kind.[9]

This passage provides us with many interesting insights into the beliefs and practices of early Christians. First, we see that Christians regularly met on a certain fixed day for worship. Second, their worship was directed to Christ, demonstrating that they firmly believed in His divinity. Furthermore, one scholar interprets Pliny's statement that hymns were sung to Christ, "as to a god," as a reference to the rather distinctive fact that, "unlike other gods who were worshipped, Christ was a person who had lived on earth." If this interpretation is correct, Pliny understood that Christians were worshipping an actual historical person as God! Of course, this agrees entirely with the

New Testament and the Biblical doctrine that Jesus was both God and man.

Not only does Pliny's letter help us understand what early Christians believed about Jesus' person, but it also reveals the high esteem to which they held His teachings. For instance, Pliny notes that Christians "bound themselves by a solemn oath" not to violate various moral standards, which find their source in the ethical teachings of Jesus. Also, Pliny's reference to the Christian custom of sharing a common meal likely alludes to their observance of communion and the "love feast." This interpretation helps explain the Christian claim that the meal was mere "food of an ordinary and innocent kind." They were attempting to counter the charge, sometimes made by non-Christians, of practicing "ritual cannibalism." The Christians of that day humbly repudiated such slanderous attacks on Jesus' teachings. We must sometimes do the same today.

There is also evidence from Jewish sources, such as Josephus in his writing *Jewish Antiquities* and writing of the Babylonian Talmud, a collection of Jewish rabbinical writings compiled between A.D. 70-200. There can be little doubt, in fact, I would say there can be NO DOUBT,

Jesus of Nazareth walked the earth and was put to death on a Roman cross. That is a historical fact! Even the most skeptical atheist must agree to that. Then the question all comes down to the claim that this Jesus rose from the dead.

This leaves us at a point, which I believe C.S. Lewis best walks us through:

> I am trying here to prevent anyone saying the really foolish thing that people often say about Him: I'm ready to accept Jesus as a great moral teacher, but I don't accept his claim to be God. That is the one thing we must not say. A man who was merely a man and said the sort of things Jesus said would not be a great moral teacher. He would either be a lunatic – on the level with the man who says he is a poached egg – or else he would be the Devil of Hell. You must make your choice. Either this man was, and is, the Son of God, or else a madman or something worse. You can shut him up for a fool, you can spit at him and kill him as a demon, or you can fall at his feet and call him Lord and God, but let us not come with any patronizing nonsense about his being a great

human teacher. He has not left that open to us. He did not intend to…Now it seems to me obvious that He was neither lunatic nor fiend: and consequently, however strange or terrifying or unlikely it may seem, I have to accept the view that He was and is God.[10]

What about you? What will you do or what have you done about your relationship with Jesus?

It is my belief, and it is precisely Biblical, that for one to live a life of meaning and fulfillment, these questions must be answered first.

4

Relationship

My search for what I am looking for brought me into a relationship with Jesus and also the ministry. I am a pastor; it is my desire for everyone to come to know and live for Jesus. I hope you would consider Jesus if you have not already done so, or think about Him again. The fact is Jesus of Nazareth walked the earth. That is an indisputable fact. Even the most agnostic or atheistic people must agree with that. What does one do with that? At this point, I hope you keep it in the back of your mind as we work forward. It is my hope and prayer that Ron's life and death, along with my own story, will "make an impact" in helping you find what you are looking for.

It is in Christ that we find out who we are and what we are living for...part of the overall purpose he is working out in everything and everyone. (Ephesians 1:11-12 MSG)

Everything, absolutely everything...got started in Christ and finds its purpose in him. (Colossians 1:16 MSG)

It is my hope and prayer that if you get only one thing out of this book, it would be that you would come to know the Lord Jesus Christ. He is the most important Man ever to live. He is God's Son. As you begin to know Him, an amazing transformation occurs. As one grows in their faith and knowledge of Jesus, they begin to understand and find exactly what it is they are looking for. One becomes part of a much larger story than living only for self. Our culture and our world simply do not tell us this; our culture and society will continually tell us it's all about you-you can and you must create your happiness.

Jesus is indeed who we are looking for. It is about a relationship with Him through faith.

> John 6:27-29, "But don't be so concerned about perishable things like food. Spend your energy seeking the eternal life that the Son of Man can give you. For God, the Father has given me the seal of his approval."
> They replied, "We want to perform God's works, too. What should we do?"
> Jesus told them, "This is the only work God wants from you: Believe in the one He has sent."

John tells us in 1 John 4:15-19:

All who confess that Jesus is the Son of God have God living in them, and they live in God. We know how much God loves us, and we have put our trust in his love. God is love, and all who live in love live in God, and God lives in them.

And as we live in God, our love grows more perfect. So we will not be afraid on the day of judgment, but we can face him with confidence because we live like Jesus here in this world.

Such love has no fear, because perfect love expels all fear. If we are afraid, it is for fear of punishment, and this shows that we have not fully experienced his perfect love. We love each other because he loved us first.

Some people have missed the most important thing in life – they don't know God. (1 Timothy 6:21 MSG)

I hope that I am using my unique experiences and gifts to impact others as I live out of my relationship with Jesus. This journey has attempted to show you how it all happened with the hope that you too will discover who you are, *whose* you are, and how you are shaped for the future. I'll bet you are gaining a pretty good idea of who you are. I believe most men do know what they're looking for; but for various reasons, we suppress or ignore the call. Some think that they are incapable; others choose not to act out of fear. Still, others are merely selfish and caught in a lifestyle of "ME FIRST." I'm sure the reasons are many, but we will never truly live until we find, accept, and embrace what we're looking for. The what is Jesus!

What do you do with all this? How do you even move towards Jesus or take action upon perhaps being convicted in all of this? One of Jesus' disciples was asked about Jesus – who He was and such, and Peter presented the Grand Narrative of Scripture and Jesus' role in the story. Acts, a book in the Bible, gives us an answer to what we should do with all of this information:

> Peter's words pierced their hearts, and they said to him and to the other apostles, "Brothers, what should we do?" Peter replied, "Each of you must repent of your sins and turn to God, and be baptized in the name of Jesus Christ for the

forgiveness of your sins. Then you will receive the gift of the Holy Spirit."   (Acts 2:37-38 NLT)

The power of God's Word draws people to Jesus, and our conscience will trouble us for the things we have done that are contrary to God's ways. We tell God we are sorry and that we do want to know and live in a relationship with Jesus. God gives us faith, the ability to know and trust Jesus. This relationship is the most important one we will ever have. A relationship with Jesus is what all people are longing for.

If we think about the search for "what I am looking for" when we think about Ron Green's life, then we may conclude; I've already found it, this is all there is, and I'm having fun, focusing on making as many skydives each day as I am able with an urgency that tomorrow it may be raining or some other reason preventing me from jumping. The mantra in skydiving circles is often along the lines of eat, drink and be merry because you only live once; have fun. I do not have anything against skydiving or any other hobby or interest; but it is my conviction that if you do not possess faith in Jesus, simply living for today will not bring fulfillment much less lasting joy and peace. The Scriptures say, "If the dead are not raised, 'Let us eat and drink, for tomorrow we die." (1 Corinthians 15:32)

Of course, this is the way far too many people live. That outlook was expressed about Ron's death in statements like, "Well, at least he went doing what he loved to do." "I'm sure if Ron had it to do all over again, he wouldn't change a thing." Tragic! If Ron truly rejected the faith of his childhood, then I know for sure that he now regrets it eternally. Living only for me is simply not enough. Something inside of you will compel you to keep searching. I have argued that the only way to find peace and contentment is through a relationship with Jesus.

I believe living merely for one's self is too small of a story. There is much more going on in the world, a much more significant story. God's Story.

LIFE IS NOT A GAME! MAKE NO MISTAKE; THIS IS SERIOUS BUSINESS!!
"See that you do not refuse the one who is speaking; for if they did not escape when they refused the one who warned

them on earth, how much less will we escape if we reject the one who warns from heaven!" (Hebrews 12:25)

5

The Church

Do you belong to any clubs or organizations? Why? It may seem like a silly question, but more than likely you desire membership in such groups to be with people who share a common interest with you. These groups may be places to learn and participate in a hobby, or they may be social, there are affinity groups of an almost limitless number. But, you choose to be a part or member correct? You see it is the same with church. The church was born and grew because people wanted to be a part of the family of God. People were drawn into a family of others who were continuing Jesus' mission of healing and restoration in the world.

The church is often perceived to be just another social club or group that individuals may choose to affiliate with. The number of different denominations and variety of churches within a community appear to offer people with a number of choices so that each person is able to find a church that fits the individual. This is exactly how most people choose a club or a place to shop etc. Our culture is a consumer-driven one in that we expect to be treated as priority number one wherever we choose to spend our hard-earned money. This same mindset is often taken into the church. People far too often look at and join churches for what they are able to get out of it, just as in any other social club or affinity group.

This is wrong. The church is different from any other group. The church is different than all others because it is a community created by God. Jesus said, "I will build my church." (Matthew 16:18) In fact, the church is Jesus' body, His presence in the world ever since He rose from the dead and ascended back to heaven. Colossians 1:18 states, "And he (Christ Jesus) is the head of the body, the church." 1 Corinthians 12:13, "For in one Spirit we were all baptized into one body – Jews or Greeks, slaves or free – and all were made to drink of one Spirit." Romans 12:4-5, "As each of us has one body with many members…so in Christ we who are many form one body."

1 Peter 2:5, "You also, like living stones, are being built into a spiritual house to be a holy priesthood, offering spiritual sacrifices acceptable to God through Jesus Christ." The church is God's gift to the world and Jesus'

continued presence among us. It should come as no surprise that as we see an increase in those who choose "none" or no church affiliation; that we also see an increase in problems in our world. Further, relativism and loss of absolute truth have risen as the church has declined.

Moreover, one of the most common questions I am asked as a pastor is, "How can I grow in my relationship with God?" It is really quite simple. And it is also where we can find what we're looking for…The Church! Jesus' Body! Think through these words:

> "Now these are the gifts Christ gave to the church: the apostles, the prophets, the evangelists, and the pastors and teachers. Their responsibility is to equip God's people to do his work and build up the church, the body of Christ." (Ephesians 4:11-12)

Martin Luther, one of the leaders of the Reformation, wrote these words in his *Large Catechism,* "Everything, therefore, in the Christian Church is ordered toward this goal: We shall daily receive in the Church nothing but the

71

forgiveness of sin through the Word and signs, to comfort and encourage our consciences as long as we live here."
Comfort and encourage, build each other up, that is the work of the Body of Christ, the Church.

Now you might cringe or be rolling your eyes at this point, but stop and think for a moment please. Jesus said that He would build the church. The church is His gift to us. Of course, it would be easy to look for problems within the church. We could look in the news and search for issues that would show us reasons to not trust the church. That would be a mistake. People are not perfect and to be sure, there are some, who choose to push an agenda or to build up self, at the expense of the church's true mission. These are easily exposed. Any church that is not completely focused on Jesus and His mission is not a true church. Jesus' final instructions were, "Therefore, go and make disciples of all the nations, baptizing them in the name of the Father and the Son and the Holy Spirit. Teach these new disciples to obey all the commands I have given you. And be sure of this: "I am with you always, even to the end of the age" (Matthew 28:19-20).

I am with you Jesus said, He works through people, through the church and His Word bringing others to Himself to be a part of His Church.

The Lutheran Church looks at the Scriptures and sees that this is entirely by the power of Jesus, it is a gift of grace. Bryan Wolfmueller, a Lutheran Church-Missouri Synod pastor writes these words:

> Once while I was patiently waiting in line to return a movie, a little lady tottered up to me and asked abruptly, "What do you do?"
>
> "I'm a Lutheran pastor."
>
> "Oh," she said. "I'm a Baptist. What's the difference?"
>
> What a surprise this conversation was!
>
> "Well," I began, "I suppose in your church, they have a time of decision at the end of the service."
>
> "Yes, an altar call."
>
> "Right, an altar call, a time to receive Jesus into your life and pray the sinner's prayer."
>
> "Yes," she said.
>
> "Lutherans do things a bit differently. Instead of asking the sinner to receive Jesus, we ask if Jesus has received us. Instead of asking the sinner to

dedicate his or her life to Christ, we ask if Christ has given His entire life and died for us. Instead of asking sinners to pray, we ask if Jesus prays for us. And the answer to this question is a sure and certain 'Yes'!"

She started crying. "That's the most wonderful thing I've ever heard."

The fact is Jesus loves you. He died on a cross for you. God's love for you is sure and certain; you cannot earn it. Nor, is there a list of "to dos" you need to check off to "get right with Him". You will receive this sure and certain love through His Word and through His Body, the Church.[11]

I challenge you to seek out a church. I, like Pastor Wolfmueller, am a Lutheran Church-Missouri Synod pastor, so I would obviously try to steer you to a LCMS church. There you will hear all about Jesus. You will experience His presence and receive His grace and mercy. I guarantee you will find exactly what it is you are looking for in the church. Jesus.

PART TWO
Growing

6

And Then What?

For the remainder of this book, there will be some short, topical, and hopefully, life applicable readings that can be read separately, like a daily devotion, or you may choose to continue reading straight through. These are intended to help you think and hopefully make or renew a living commitment to Jesus our Lord and Savior, to grow in relationship with Him. These next two sections, Part Two and Three are best experienced with others. Consider working through them with your spouse, family, or a small group. Ultimately, these are included to help you find what you are looking for. Blessings to you as you think through these selections.

There is still time…

> Long ago God spoke many times and in many ways to our ancestors through the prophets. And

now in these final days, he has spoken to us through his Son. God promised everything to the Son as an inheritance, and through the Son, he created the universe. The Son radiates God's own glory and expresses the very character of God, and he sustains everything by the mighty power of his command. When he had cleansed us from our sins, he sat down in the place of honor at the right hand of the majestic God in heaven. This shows that the Son is far greater than the angels, just as the name God gave him is greater than their names. (Hebrews 1:1-4 NLT)

It is indeed all about Jesus! The Old Testament in the Bible points to Jesus, and the New Testament speaks of Jesus' time walking this earth.

We must pay more careful attention, therefore, to what we have heard, so that we do not drift away. For if the message spoken by angels was binding, and every violation and disobedience received its just punishment, how shall we escape if we ignore such a great salvation? This salvation, which was first announced by the Lord, was confirmed to us by those who heard him. (Hebrews 2:1-3 NIV)

Time is our most precious resource. The title of this book is *There is still Time;* however, our time on earth is finite, and I believe that we are to use and spend that time wisely. The acronym T.I.M.E. is explained in T.I.M.E. # 1 below. It is a helpful way for us to use our time intelligently.

T.I.M.E. #1

TIME

Among the legendary stories about Abraham Lincoln is the account of his visit to a slave auction. He went to observe, not to participate. He watched the unspeakable indignities of selling and buying human beings. His response was a mixture of disgust, sadness, and outrage.

As he stood there, a young woman was brought to the block, her eyes and body language screaming defiance and hatred. She had been used and abused by her previous owners, and now it was going to happen all over again.

The bidding began, and to everyone's amazement, Lincoln offered a bid. As the price went up, so did Lincoln's bids until the auctioneer declared him the buyer. He paid her price and then went over to where she was being held. All her animosity was focused squarely on him. He looked at her and simply said, "You're free." Dripping defiance and distrust, she said, "Yeah, free for what?" Abraham Lincoln answered, "Free to do anything you want to do; free to go anywhere you want to go." Her appearance changed as she took in his words and realized he meant what he said. Lincoln repeated himself: "You're free . . . free to go anywhere you want to go." She answered, "then I'm going with you!"

What a response! I am sure that this woman had no idea her fate that day. Imagine her bitterness toward living in slavery only to find out that she is now free. Of course, it is no different for us. We are all slaves who have been set free from the bondage of sin, death, and the devil through Jesus' paying for our release through His death on a cross. Our response must be the same as the young lady in our story, "Then I'm going with you!" I will follow you, Lord, because you have bought and redeemed me. I AM FREE!

But use your freedom wisely, for good. 1 Peter 2:9-10, "But you are a chosen people, a royal priesthood, a holy nation, a people belonging to God, that you may declare the praises of him who called you out of darkness into his wonderful light." Later in verse 16, "Live as people who are free, not using your freedom as a cover-up for evil, but living as servants of God."

People belonging to God should live as exiles in the world that rejects God's message. We bear witness to the gospel when we live in a way that pleases God. Too often though, we live to please ourselves.

TIME

Each of us has been given enough time to accomplish God's purpose for
us on this planet. The Scriptures exhort us to invest our time wisely, reminding us that God determines the length of our stay on earth. "Therefore, be careful how you walk, not as unwise men, but as wise, making the most of your time, because the days are evil" (Ephesians 5:15-16). Toward the end of his life, Moses prayed, "So teach us to count our days, that we may gain a wise heart" (Psalm 90:12).

Time is our most valuable asset, but without a proper perspective, we will spend it foolishly. A biblical perspective on time involves several things:

(1) Life is brief, and we cannot be presumptuous about the future (see James 4:14).

(2) The eternal gives meaning to the temporal (see Romans 13:11; 2 Corinthians 4:18).

(3) Like other assets, our time is owned by God (see Psalm 31:15).

(4) We must be sensitive to opportunities so that we can make the most of them (see Ecclesiastes 8:5; Colossians 4:5).

(5) Our use of time will reflect our priorities (see Matthew 6:19-21,34).

Just as it is wise to budget our financial resources, it is also wise to plan our use of time. Most time is wasted not in hours, but in minutes. If we do not regularly assess the way we spend our 168 hours per week, our schedules will get cluttered with activities that may be good, but not the best. How much quality time do we spend with the Lord, with our spouse, with our children, and with our non-Christian friends? God wants us to be faithful stewards, not squanderers, of the time He has given us.

Carefully evaluate your weekly use of time by filling in a

168- hour worksheet as accurately as possible. What areas need to be trimmed down, and where should you be spending more of your time?

Assessment of how can I increase or live TIME?
In Luke 7, we hear a story of response to living as God's chosen. In fact, we see two responses in this story, a grateful penitent response and an envious, self-centered response. Luke 7 beginning in verse 36:

"Now one of the Pharisees invited Jesus to have dinner with him, so he went to the Pharisee's house and reclined at the table."

It is significant to note that Jesus accepts an invitation to the house of a Pharisee when considering the opposition He faced from them as a whole. Jesus is willing to accept us even if we've rejected Him in the past.

> When a woman who had lived a sinful life (most likely a prostitute or an adulteress) in that town learned that Jesus was eating at the Pharisee's house, she brought an alabaster jar of perfume, and as she stood behind him at his feet weeping,

she began to wet his feet with her tears. Then she wiped them with her hair, kissed them and poured perfume on them. (Luke 7:37-38)

This woman who seemingly had no business being in the presence of these holy men offers an act of hospitality withheld by Simon, the self-righteous Pharisee.

"When the Pharisee who had invited him saw this, he said to himself, 'If this man were a prophet, he would know who is touching him and what kind of woman she is--that she is a sinner.'" (Luke 7:39)

If an impure person like this touched an observant Jew, he would be unable to enter the temple area, celebrate festivals, or offer sacrifices. But, Jesus not only knows what is going on here, but He also reveals He is a true prophet by revealing what is in Simon's heart.

Jesus answered him, "Simon, I have something to tell you." "Tell me, teacher," he said. "Two men owed money to a certain moneylender. One owed him five hundred denarii, and the other fifty. Neither of them had the money to pay him back, so he canceled the debts of both. Now which of them will love him more?" Simon replied, "I suppose the one who had the bigger debt canceled." "You have judged correctly,"

Then he turned toward the woman and said to Simon, "Do you see this woman? I came into your house. You did not give me any water for my feet, but she wet my feet with her tears and wiped them with her hair.

You did not give me a kiss, but this woman, from the time I entered, has not stopped kissing my feet. You did not put oil on my head, but she has poured perfume on my feet." (Luke 7:40-46)

Ordinary hospitality at this time included the opportunity to wash, and the kiss of greeting would be comparable to a reception with a handshake today. Simon didn't offer any form of hospitality.

"Therefore, I tell you, her many sins have been forgiven-- for she loved much. But he who has been forgiven little loves little." (Luke 7:47)

This woman's love did not earn her forgiveness of sins; it was a response, an outpouring of gratitude to Jesus' mercy. The Pharisee most likely felt that he was without sin and indeed would not receive anything from Jesus.

> Then Jesus said to her, "Your sins are forgiven." The other guests began to say among themselves, "Who is this who even forgives sins?" Jesus said to the woman, "Your faith has saved you; go in peace." (Luke 7:49-50)

There are no spoken words by the woman recorded in our story, yet we see her repentance; her realization of who she is in relation to who Jesus is. The people are shocked because only God can forgive sins.

What a response! Both of the debtors in Jesus' parable were sinners in need of forgiveness. The obvious sinner, the woman needed forgiveness, but so did Simon, the Pharisee. We are all sinners; every one of us needs Jesus' forgiveness.

One was dutiful, at best, while the other responded out of love and gratitude. As I think about this story, I wonder what my response would be? What about you? Jesus forgives, saves, and restores us. Do we respond in love through faith, service, and following Jesus? Or, do we respond as a Pharisee, out of duty and obligation, not seeing Jesus for who He is or completely grasping what He has done for us?

So, here's the difficult part I believe. It is impossible really, to tell somebody how to love. Think about it for a moment. If we look closely at these two stories, it is clear that the response of giving and serving through love is the better one, isn't it? We know the Scriptures tell us we are to love Jesus with all our heart, soul, mind and strength.

How do we tell/teach somebody to do that? Are we able to tell somebody else how to love his or her spouse or kids? No. That's the whole point of this entire message, I believe. We can offer some ideas and specifics I suppose, but then it becomes a duty. Well, you should give your money to Jesus, you should sign up to serve in Jesus' church, maybe if you served at a soup kitchen, then you'll be expressing love to Jesus. If others follow through on these suggestions out of obligation or duty, it is not love.

In fact, the opposite can and does occur, and one can become resentful.

True love, the responses of love as shown by the woman only flows from a deep sense of gratitude in realizing who we are and also realizing who Jesus is and what He has done for us. This is only possible through a relationship, through knowing Him.

Think about our earthly relationships. Think about first being married, or the birth of your children. Didn't you just respond as the woman in our story today, pouring out gifts, loving them because of who they are? It is merely a response of love. You spent time together; you simply could not get enough of each other. Problems only arise when we turn the focus off of the other and put it on ourselves. What happened to my time? I used to have money to buy a new parachute or motorcycle every year. Now I'm driving an eleven-year-old vehicle. Poor me! I start functioning out of duty.

I cannot tell you how to love. No one can really. If we focus on the relationship though, we will come to love the Lord because we cannot help but realize all He has done for us and continues to do. We are filled with the peace that surpasses all human understanding. We respond through love.

So, I came up with this little acronym a few years ago. It's an acronym that works for any relationship, but specifically for our relationship with Jesus. Use it often to find what you are looking for. It is **T.I.M.E.**

To, invest, minutes, everyday.

To is a reminder to think of the other. Think about writing out a tag on a gift, or a letter; it is to, to someone else, not me. When we do this, the focus is moved to the other, and that is a good thing. It is difficult to listen or offer our focused-attention when occupied with self.

Invest is vital because invest implies that it is an intentional effort on our part. We are in touch, engaged, not merely sitting; or perhaps not only putting in our one hour on Sunday morning, investing versus spending time. No, we are investing in the relationship. How often are we intentional in using our time as an investment?

Minutes remind us to spend quality time. It does take time to get to know someone. It also takes time to continue and grow a relationship. We cannot simply begin a relationship and then coast, or the relationship will dry up. Further, investing minutes involves giving of oneself to the other.

Everyday is closely related to minutes in that it must be every day. When we do the first three, the every day part becomes easy because focusing on the relationship becomes a priority. Much like the woman in our story, we crave time with the Lord; it becomes as oxygen, food, and water to us. We cannot live without Him.

T.I.M.E.

Praise be to the God and Father of our Lord Jesus Christ! In his great mercy he has given us new birth into a living hope through the resurrection of Jesus Christ from the dead, and into an inheritance that can never perish, spoil or fade--kept in heaven for you, who through faith are shielded by God's power until the coming of the salvation that is ready to be revealed in the last time. In this, you greatly rejoice, though now for a little while you may have had to suffer grief in all kinds of trials. These have come so that your faith--of greater worth than gold, which perishes even though refined by fire--may be proved genuine and may result in praise, glory, and honor when Jesus Christ is revealed.

Though you have not seen him, you love him; and even though you do not see him now, you believe in him and are filled with an inexpressible and glorious joy, for you are receiving the goal of your faith, the salvation of your souls. (1 Peter 1:3-9 NIV)

T.I.M.E. # 2

That Others May Live…

In August of 1943, 21 persons bailed out of a disabled C-46 over an uncharted jungle near the China-Burma border. So remote was the crash site that the only means of getting help to the survivors was by Para drop. Lieutenant Colonel Don Fleckinger and two medical corpsmen volunteered for the assignment. For a month these men, aided by natives, cared for the injured until the party was brought to safety. News commentator Eric Severeid was one of the men to survive this ordeal. He later wrote of the men who risked their lives to save him: "Gallant is a precious word; they deserve it."

From this event the need for a highly trained rescue force was found; thus, Air Force Pararescue was brought into being. Rescues since then have occurred in virtually every corner of the world. Since that first rescue, many airmen, soldiers, and civilians have had firsthand experience that when trouble strikes, PARARESCUEMEN are ready to come to their aid.

Roughly two thousand years ago, God sent his Son into enemy territory; a world broken, separated from God because of sin.

"But your iniquities have separated you from your God; your sins have hidden his face from you so that he will not hear. For your hands are stained with blood, your fingers with guilt. Your lips have spoken lies, and your tongue mutters wicked things." (Isaiah 59:2-3)

"But when the time had fully come, God sent his Son, born of a woman, born under the law, that we might receive the full rights of sons." (Galatians 4:4)

"For God so loved the world that he gave his one and only Son," (John 3:16)

The Pararescue motto is "It is my duty as a Pararescueman to save life and aid injured. I will be prepared at all times to perform my assigned duties quickly and efficiently, placing these duties before personal desires and comforts. These things I do, that others may live..."

The apostle John said, "And we have seen and testify that the Father has sent his Son to be the Savior of the world." (1 John 4:14)

Jesus said, "For I did not come to judge the world, but to save it." (John 12:47)

I suppose it is no secret or surprise to you by now that I tend to see the world through a "military" lens. I cannot help myself, but I believe the Scriptures certainly lend themselves to this. There is a battle going on, and we are in the midst of it. Yes, Air Force Pararescue has "saved" many people throughout their existence. But, this obviously pales by comparison to the numbers and type of "saving" done by our Lord and Savior Jesus Christ. His entire mission was "That others may live..."

Now perhaps I am "preaching to the choir" here with Christianity 101 right? Most, if not all of us know that Jesus is the Savior sent to save us from our sins. Do we need to go over this again? I believe the answer to that is yes. But, first, if we look more closely, I believe we are essentially being given the same challenge as Joshua gave the nation of Israel. Joshua reminded the people of the

Lord's deliverance, provision and the promised land, which they would now possess. Joshua asks the people to choose whom they will serve. Who will they trust to give them life? Jesus is saying unless we feed on his flesh and blood we will not live. What does this mean? In a nutshell, Jesus is saying, "I am the way and the truth and the life," (John 14:6) there is no other way.

The people to whom the Pararescue are sent are desperate and without hope, except for the team who attempt to come in and save them. I rather doubt that any would say, 'no thanks I'll go ahead and get out on my own.' And yet, as ridiculous as this sounds, people do this all the time to Jesus. In fact, that is what the World's Religions are saying to Jesus' way. I suppose that broadly religions can be separated into "works righteousness" or "fatalistic" groupings. Islam, for example, requires people to perform specific acts and rituals to satisfy Allah. Buddhism would be on the other side, saying that it doesn't matter, this life is all there is, and when it is over, we will just return to the eternal energy.

And then I am reminded of the people of Israel; they were in a covenant relationship with God and yet needed warning over and over again. The Bible presents many prophets and leaders of God's people to remember the Lord's deliverance and provision. We are probably no different, are we? I don't know about you, but I need a daily reminder, most times more than daily, that Jesus gave Himself entirely for you and me. There is indeed nothing that I can do to restore my broken relationship with God; it is entirely outside of me just like a parachute. Jesus paid the price for my sins and your sins, and he has given us eternal life with Him. That is the hope that is in us! Why do we sometimes try to rely on our abilities thinking that it is all about us?

One day I was in Tennessee skydiving just for fun with a large group. It was busy, and jumpers were to be ready at the loading area because the airplane never turned off, it just went up dropped a load and came immediately back for the next. While standing with a group visiting and waiting for the airplane, we noticed that people were beginning to look up into the air and point at a jumper. As the jumper neared the ground, we saw that he was in a slow turn to the right. As he became closer and closer to the ground people started yelling, PULL, PULL! Well, he never did. He impacted the ground in the same slow right turn that he seemed to be in the entire jump.

As it turns out he was an inexperienced jumper who only recently progressed out of student status. The real tragedy was that this jumper was equipped with an automatic opener on his reserve. It was OFF.

On a different day, I had an advanced student requiring only me as a jumpmaster. This student was working on spotting the airplane (looking out the open door straight down at the ground below to determine the exit point) and a few other air skills on this particular jump. After spotting the aircraft the student dove headfirst out of the plane and then assumed the face-to-earth stable position as directed. After an altitude check, the student was to turn and "track" away from me. Tracking is a technique, which jumpers use to cover large amounts of ground while jumping, as well as to move to clear air away from other jumpers when nearing opening altitude.

Well, this student turned and tracked and tracked and tracked. I couldn't believe it; further, it didn't seem like this guy was even aware of his altitude. As opening altitude approached, I decided that I should remind the student that it was time to stop and open his parachute. I could barely catch him long enough to grab his leg and tapped his ripcord as a reminder to open NOW. After this, I had to open my parachute because we were getting mighty low. As soon as I opened, I looked around and noticed that not too far below me was my student hanging under his reserve parachute. You see these students also are required to wear automatic opening devices on their reserves in case something like this happens. Saved! This guy was free to roam the wild blue yonder without care, and he ended up fine. What a lesson.

We are saved! I believe that we are only able to fly off into the wild blue yonder living free when we know that our automatic opener Jesus is with us. He did it all for us. We are saved by grace through faith, and we see with new eyes knowing Him, and the Holy Spirit empowers us. We are free to live the life we were created to live. Why would anyone reject His grace choosing to live their own way, in the dark, refusing to come to the light spending their entire lives going in a slow circle to nowhere until the day they die?

T.I.M.E. #3
Brace for Impact

Your outlook on life changes after you've ridden a powerless jetliner toward the icy Hudson River and hear a voice over the intercom: "This is the captain. Brace for impact."

You change your priorities. You lose interest in life's little dramas. Yes, one gets a whole new perspective on life.

Shortly after US Airways flight 1549 took off from LaGuardia Airport at 3:26 p.m. on January 15, 2009, it flew through a flock of geese knocking out both engines. Gliding at only approximately 2800 ft. over New York City Captain Chesley "Sully" Sullenberger and First Officer Jeff Skiles began a turn in an attempt to return to LaGuardia. Well, most of us remember that Sully noticed the Hudson River and realized that their best hopes of survival were to try and land in the river. They were successful, and all 155 souls were saved. Some of these survivors meet to mark the anniversary and remember their "second chance" in life; indeed, every one of them was changed in some way.

Brace for impact! What a statement! For the people of Flight 1549, it is an immediate wake-up call and call to action, to remember their second chance on life, a call to remember the essential things in life. The entire Scriptures are essentially saying the same regarding Jesus. "Brace for impact" the Savior is coming, and He will impact the world. We're waiting for the Promised-One who will come into the world to rescue it. The entire Old Testament was telling the People of God to brace for impact. For example, in Isaiah 61, God states that He will send the Messiah into the world. You will know who he is because he will proclaim the good news, bind up the brokenhearted and release the prisoners from darkness. He will suffer humiliation, be tortured and die for the sins of all people. Everyone is given a second chance with God.

And now we wait too. We brace for impact as we wait to celebrate and remember that God, in fact, did fulfill this promise in sending Jesus to save His creation. But, that's not the end; we cannot stop at the birth and arrival of Jesus, as awesome and amazing as that is. No, we're ultimately Easter People. Because of Jesus' death and resurrection; we too wait. We also wait for the return of the King. Acts 2:11 states, "Men of Galilee," they said, "why do you stand here looking into the sky? This same Jesus, who has been taken from you into heaven, will come back in the same way you have seen him go into heaven."

So, we celebrate and remember God's promise and fulfilling of the Old Covenant, and we live in the New Covenant by the power of the Holy Spirit. But we brace for impact as well waiting for Jesus to come back into the world to complete the task of restoration that He began and continues even now to work through His body the church. **What are your priorities?** He will help you to see what is most important in life. In fact, He gives all people a second chance at life.

The reality is, we all need to 'Brace for Impact.' **What would change for you today, if you were on Flight 1549 and the pilot called, Brace for Impact?**

Hold that thought as we look in the Scriptures at Jesus' disciple's reaction to their moment of Impact with the Lord. It's a look at the reaction of Jesus' closest followers, the ones who knew the Scriptures and the stories of the people of God and their waiting. They were living in the fulfillment of the Old Covenant.

It's the resurrection story; we're joining this story after Jesus has conquered death and left the tomb. He has just finished visiting with and teaching two of His followers walking to Emmaus, and they went to tell the disciples. Verse 36:

> While they were saying all this, Jesus appeared to them and said, "Peace be with you." They thought they were seeing a ghost and were scared half to death. He continued with them, "Don't be upset and don't let all these doubting questions take over. Look at my hands, look at my feet – it's really me. Touch me. Look me over from head to toe. A ghost doesn't have muscle and bone like this." As he said this, he showed them his hands and feet. They still couldn't believe what they were seeing. It was too much; it seemed too good to be true.
>
> He asked, "Do you have any food here?" They gave him a piece of leftover fish they had cooked. He took it and ate it right before their eyes.

Then he said, "Everything I told you while I was with you comes to this: All the things written about me in the Law of Moses, in the Prophets, and in the Psalms have to be fulfilled." He went on to open their understanding of the Word of God, showing them how to read their Bibles this way. He said, "You can see now how it is written that the Messiah suffers, rises from the dead on the third day, and then a total life-change through the forgiveness of sins is proclaimed in his name to all nations – starting from here, from Jerusalem." (Luke 24:36-47 MSG)

Jesus is uniquely qualified for this mission. He is the one sent by God to open a new way of living as God's people. No doubt, the Scriptures talked about here included the Suffering Servant reading from Isaiah 53:6 "All of us, like sheep, have strayed away. We have left God's paths to follow our own. Yet the Lord laid on him the sins of us all." The second chance. Only Jesus could pull this off because He was sinless, He would pay for all people, and

He would conquer death. As the Scriptures foretold, Jesus told the disciples to brace for impact. He was going to suffer and die, "be ready; it has to be this way; in fact, it's the only way." Only the Son of God is equipped and qualified to complete the mission. They all fled, they left the Lord! And now: **A Second Chance, forgiveness of sins – freedom!**

Sully was also uniquely qualified to pull off that landing, which many called a miracle. In a later interview, Sully stated that he places a tremendously high value on human life. Chesley Sullenberger was an Air Force Academy graduate and F-4 fighter pilot. Twelve of his fellow F-4 pilots died in training exercises, which impacted him significantly. He decided to study the crashes in an attempt to learn why they occurred so that he would hopefully be able to save not only his own life but also the lives of others.

His findings were really quite remarkable and pointed to a truth that lies within all people. What was the cause or reason for these fatalities? The pilots waited too long to eject. They worked too long believing they could solve the problem instead of ejecting to safety. Rather than facing the embarrassment of losing a multi-million-dollar aircraft, they perished attempting to save it. Only Sully knows what he was thinking that day and why he decided to try a water landing, which is part of basic pilot training.

Interesting, isn't it? How many of us can relate? Not being willing to admit a mistake, attempting to solve our own problems, realizing that we are in over our heads and cannot fix the situation without intervention. Unwilling, for whatever reason, to accept a second chance. It takes the finality of 'Brace for Impact' for us too often, doesn't it?

A total life-change! It's just too good to be true, just as surviving Flight 1549.

Jesus was alive, but His disciples didn't believe it. They doubted the Son of God. Jesus restored their faith by revealing Himself to them. And He forgave their unbelief. Now what? What will they do with their second chance? What will be the result of their total "life-change"?

"You're the first to hear and see it. You're the witnesses. What comes next is very important: I am sending what my

Father promised to you, so stay here in the city until he arrives until you're equipped with power from on high."

Now you will go out and tell people to Brace for Impact. You will be equipped to offer my gift of a second chance because of who I am, Jesus said. People will be free to live for me.

What would change for you today, if you were on Flight 1549 and the pilot called, Brace for Impact? That's our gift today. Just as Isaiah told the people to brace for impact, the Savior is coming; we remember that that prophecy was fulfilled in Jesus. Now we need to brace for impact ourselves – live for Him; He is returning. We need to tell others, brace for impact Jesus is Lord, and He is returning – repent and live for Him.

One can only imagine the shock and terror of being told to brace for impact! What do you think would come into your mind? Especially if one had a few minutes to ponder as did the members of flight 1549. If only…If only I had done…The shock must have been the same for the disciples seeing the Suffering Servant story from Isaiah unfold before their very eyes. Imagine their fear and terror, they all fled!

Imagine the incredible feeling of being given a second chance! The people of Flight 1549 no longer take life for granted. The Lord forgave the disciples; they were empowered from on high, His Holy Spirit within them to go and share this incredible story with the world.

This is OUR Story! This same Suffering Servant offers us the same forgiveness. We receive the same Holy Spirit; we're a part of Jesus' Body as well. We're to build each other up, do our part of preparing and then we're sent. We're sent out to tell the world to Brace for Impact. Jesus is coming back, live for Him. JUST Like the disciples and the members of Flight 1549, we must act! We cannot hold back, attempting to pull this off on our own. Do you need to make a new beginning? Are you giving Jesus complete control? Do you need to look at your priorities? Perhaps, re-prioritize? We also must take this message to the world. How will you do that? We have so many opportunities to live for Jesus.

T.I.M.E. #4
Searching for Identity

Do you like bumper stickers, or it seems that these days, window stickers are becoming the thing? You know the ones? I think one of the first I noticed was the silhouette of a hockey player. Now you can get many different types of sports, pictures of the family, mom, dad, the kids, dog, and cat even. Of course, there's also the old standard with some written message. I remember a time in my own life when I boldly shared who I was on the back windows of my pickup truck. It is interesting to me that these stickers are really an identification or identity, aren't they? I mean they show who we are and we proudly display them. We see it in the hats we wear and the messaged t-shirts too. We are people who crave an identity. We want others to know who we are and the issues that are important to us. These identities might fit us and make us happy for a time, but the only identity that will genuinely fulfill and give us lasting peace is as a Child of God. It's true, but let's move on for now.

Consider this story from the Scriptures. The people of God had been delivered out of the bondage of slavery in

Egypt and were preparing to enter the land God had brought them to; they were supposed to be proudly identifying themselves with Him. They were to live as His ambassador in the Promised Land living entirely for Him and influencing others because of their identity. Listen to what the Lord told Moses before Moses' death and the people of God entering the Land.

> See, I have set before you today life and prosperity, death and destruction. For I command you today to love the Lord your God, to walk in obedience to him, and to keep his commands, decrees, and laws; then you will live and increase, and the Lord your God will bless you in the land you are entering to possess. But if your heart turns away and you are not obedient, and if you are drawn away to bow down to other gods and worship them, I declare to you this day that you will certainly be destroyed. You will not live long in the land you are crossing the Jordan to enter and possess. This day I call the heavens and the earth as witnesses against you that I have set before you life and death, blessings and curses. Now choose life, so that you and your children may live and

that you may love the Lord your God, listen to his voice and hold fast to him. For the Lord is your life, and he will give you many years in the land he swore to give to your fathers, Abraham, Isaac, and Jacob. (Deuteronomy 30:15-20 NIV)

The people of God went through good and bad times as described throughout the Old Testament. Prophets would show them their sinful ways, remind them of their identity and call them to turn back to God, they would repent and live as God's people for a time, but then they would fall away through the influence of the pagans in their midst. Ultimately, as predicted by the Lord, they were taken away into captivity; removed from the Promised Land, seemingly forever excluded from God's glorious presence.

Even though they were in exile, the Lord would not forget His people. Yet though they had forgotten who they were, He did not. He continued to love them and call them to repent and turn to Him. Ezekiel was one of these prophets of the Lord, and he spoke to the Jews who were captive in Babylon. He is perhaps the least understood of the prophets due to the unusual method in which the Lord had him deliver His message. Ezekiel modeled or mirrored the actions of the people of God providing unforgettable and even shocking portrayals, which would wake them up and show them how they had failed as God's people. Psalm 137 describes this time for the people of God.

"By the rivers of Babylon, we sat and wept when we remembered Zion...How can we sing songs of the Lord while in a foreign land?" (V. 1-2 NIV)

The Bible book of Ezekiel opens with "while I was among the exiles by the Kebar River," which is a river that flowed through Babylon. The Psalm describes the crushed spirit of the people of God and the apparent hopelessness of their situation. The significant part of the first half of Ezekiel is spent presenting the sinfulness of the people, which had gone on for generations and God's wrath against them because of it. God's passionate desire was to reveal Himself to those captives through this prophet. The message of Ezekiel's life is to remember there is hope when you focus on God's glory. Through Ezekiel's dramatic object lessons the people were reminded that God is alive and He is at work. He has never stopped loving His people. God is sovereign and Holy; God's grace is not earned, but there are terms of the relationship. Those

114

terms are spelled out in God's Law. The people believed that the promises of God were guaranteed regardless of their transgressions forgetting who God is and who they are in relation to Him.

Later in Ezekiel, the Lord reminds them and again offers His amazing grace:

> "Therefore, O house of Israel, I will judge you, each one according to his ways, declares the Sovereign Lord. Repent! Turn away from all your offenses; then sin will not be your downfall. Rid yourselves of all the offenses you have committed, and get a new heart and a new spirit. Why will you die, O house of Israel? For I take no pleasure in the death of anyone, declares the Sovereign Lord. Repent and live!" (Ezekiel 18:30-32 NIV)

What is your identity? What sticker have you in your window? Your identity is of significant importance in your search to what you are looking for. Have you ever been intentional and considered that your search might begin with your identity in relation to your Creator?

Nothing much has changed with people throughout time has it? We are born in the same condition as the People of God in Ezekiel's day. We are children of Adam and Eve, sinners. We forget who we are and whose we are. Thankfully though, our amazing God does not change either. Fortunately, what has changed though, is the terms of our relationship with God. Through establishing the new covenant, we are offered a new heart and a new spirit (Ezekiel 36). We CAN change, or the Lord God can change us.

> So the law was our guardian until Christ came that we might be justified by faith. Now that this faith has come, we are no longer under a guardian. So in Christ Jesus, you are all children of God through faith, for all of you who were baptized into Christ have clothed yourselves with Christ. (Galatians 3:24-27 NIV)

> But when the set time had fully come, God sent his Son, born of a woman, born under the law, to redeem those under the law, that we might receive adoption to sonship. Because you are his sons, God sent the Spirit of his Son into our heart, the

Spirit who calls out, 'Abba Father.' So you are no longer a slave, but God's child; and since you are his child, God has made you also an heir. (Galatians 4:4-7 NIV)

A child of God! What an identity! If one considers the message of Ezekiel in these terms, it is pretty easy to see why our world is the way it is. People are lost searching for an identity. Some strive to be great doctors, lawyers, auto mechanics, and whatever profession and that is their identity. Those are wonderful and even essential identities, but they are incomplete. Others search by filling other roles, great dad, mom, son, daughter, or grandma, but it isn't enough. Some don't even know where to search, or they get tired trying on different ones, so try to lose the identity that they portray through means such as drugs, alcohol, pornography, unhealthy relationships, etc. The gods of this world are many, and none will ever give us the lasting identity we need.

I think we are pretty good about boldly proclaiming this fact and speaking of grace in our churches if you happen to belong to or attend one. I think maybe where we come up a bit short is in proclaiming the truths of which, Ezekiel spoke. God is holy, sovereign and just. Grace wouldn't be such a big deal if there were no wrath of God. Yes, identity as a child of God is incredible, but we are to love the Lord with all our heart, mind, soul, and strength just like the people of God in Ezekiel's time. We are to love our neighbors as ourselves too. We are to live entirely in our identity as children of God. Galatians 6:7 says, "Do not be deceived: God cannot be mocked. A man reaps what he sows." Yes, there are terms to our covenant too.

Once clothed with this identity through our baptism and faith, we receive the power of the Holy Spirit to help us live within the covenant. Nourished by the means of Grace, the Word, and the Lord's Supper, we are strengthened to live in our identity as children of God. And when we sin, we can return to the Lord asking for and receiving forgiveness by His grace.

> The Spirit helps us in our weakness. We do not know what we ought to pray for, but the Spirit himself intercedes for us through wordless groans. And he who searches our hearts knows the mind of the Spirit because the Spirit intercedes for God's people in accordance with the will of God. And

we know that in all things God works for the good of those who love him, who have been called according to his purpose. (Romans 8:26-28 NIV)

Forgive my bit or preaching; however, I genuinely believe that the search for what we are looking for must begin with our Creator. We must know "Whose" we are before we can consider "Who" we are and discover what we are looking for. I hope and pray that this becomes clearer as we journey together.

T.I.M.E. #5

All In

In the final poker scene in the James Bond movie *Casino Royale,* we see an intense battle of wills. Four players are engaged in a high-stakes game that has the entire casino locked-in, watching in anticipation as the game unfolds, a game that is a metaphor for the actual battle about to take place between James and the villain. The bets are ridiculously high, the pot climbing into the millions of dollars. In the final hand, all four players possess decent cards that would win many games. Two of the players go All In during final bets, as James and the villain boldly raise, bringing the total over $115 million. Tension mounts as each player, in turn, reveals their winning hand, only to be bested by the next. Finally, James, our hero, lays down the straight flush the highest hand in poker. The villain storms out of the room and the viewer is prepared for the climactic scene, which will soon take place between our two players. In essence, we see that both James and the villain are "All In" as well for what remains in the movie.

ALL IN! What a great statement. In poker, "all in" is the term used when a player desires to "call," but does not have enough money to do so to match the amount of the current raise in the bet. However, the player believes he has a winning hand and desires to remain in the game; he does not want to fold. All In, the player gives everything, all his money to keep playing; even when he does not have enough money to call.

What a great metaphor for faith and our relationship with the Lord! We do not have enough; there is absolutely nothing we can do to stay in the game. We cannot do anything; Jesus has the winning hand so to speak. He has paid our price, dying and rising from the dead to secure the ultimate Prize. We can never pay enough for this on our own. The only thing we can do, by the power of the Holy Spirit, is to live ALL IN. We give our entire heart, mind, and soul to the Lord by faith to join in this life with Jesus. How?

We see the people of the early church in Acts going ALL IN, as they sell their possessions and work together to live in a community of faith. It seems that their entire existence is lived out in response to the miraculous work of Jesus' winning hand! They are consumed with living for Jesus because of all that He has done. Let's take time today to reflect on our lives and prepare to go ALL IN.

In the book of Acts, we see how events unfolded after Jesus' resurrection and we see the birth and growth of the church. Peter and John appear to be the ones who were first teaching and speaking of what they had witnessed in Jesus' death and resurrection. They used Scripture to show that Jesus was the one predicted to come, the Messiah who would once and for all restore the Kingdom of Israel. They would later learn that those who put their faith and trust in Jesus now defined the Kingdom of Israel. It was no longer a national Kingdom.

Just before our reading for consideration, Peter and John were arrested for spreading the message of Jesus. The Holy Spirit was working powerfully through them as they were able to heal, but more importantly, God used their message to "cut people to the heart." Many recognized their own sins and were told to repent and to turn to God for the forgiveness of sins. The number was already 5000.

"Now when they saw the boldness of Peter and John and realized that they were uneducated and ordinary men, they were amazed and recognized them as companions of Jesus." (Acts 4:13 NIV)

Peter and John were warned to stop teaching about Jesus so that the spread of the message would end, but they answered, "Which is right in God's eyes: to listen to you, or to him? You are the judges! As for us, we cannot help speaking about what we have seen and heard." (Acts 4:19-20 NIV) What boldness to the authorities! They are ALL IN!

After further threats, they are let go. They returned to the people who pray for boldness. They prayed for boldness and the place shook by the power of the Lord and they became even bolder. The world's response to the message of Jesus is persecution and the early church models for us what should be the appropriate response, prayers. At this point, we also get a glimpse how they lived ALL IN. The book of Acts 4:36:

"Joseph, a Levite from Cyprus, whom the apostles called Barnabas (which means "son of encouragement"), sold a field he owned and brought the money and put it at the apostle's feet."

Here we have an example of living ALL IN, a voluntary act given out of gratitude and thanksgiving for what Jesus had done. It is interesting that immediately following this positive example, we are given an example of hypocrisy. Instead of ALL IN giving and living, we are presented with a graphic picture of trying to deceive the Lord.

> Acts Chapter 5:
> Now a man named Ananias, together with his wife Sapphira, also sold a piece of property. With his wife's full knowledge he kept back part of the money for himself, but brought the rest and put it at the apostles' feet. Then Peter said, "Ananias, how is it that Satan has so filled your heart that you have lied to the Holy Spirit and have kept for yourself some of the money you received for the land? Didn't it belong to you before it was sold? And after it was sold, wasn't the money at your disposal? What made you think of doing such a thing? You have not lied to men but to God."

When Ananias heard this, he fell down and died. And great fear seized all who heard what had happened. Then the young men came forward, wrapped up his body, and carried him out and buried him. About three hours later his wife came in, not knowing what had happened. Peter asked her, "Tell me, is this the price you and Ananias got for the land?"

"Yes," she said, "that is the price." Peter said to her, "How could you agree to test the Spirit of the Lord? Look! The feet of the men who buried your husband are at the door, and they will carry you out also." At that moment she fell down at his feet and died. Then the young men came in and, finding her dead, carried her out and buried her beside her husband. Great fear seized the whole church and all who heard about these events. (Acts 5:1-11 NIV)

The great deceiver loves to tell us lies about our relationship with the Lord. One can only imagine how the devil worked to deceive Ananias and Sapphira. "You do not need to go ALL IN; you can become great in the eyes of the world, you will gain a favorable reputation through being a part of this community of faith." They apparently loved material possessions more than the Lord.

It is important to note that the land was theirs, they did not have to give any of the money to the church. The sin was in deceiving and lying to God, not men. They wanted to be loved by the world and in its ways more than they wanted to surrender to God completely.

God wants our whole heart. Remember when Jesus was asked which is the greatest commandment?

"Love the Lord your God with all your heart and with all your soul and with all your mind. This is the first and greatest commandment." (Matthew 22:37)

The threats and challenges to living ALL IN are both external, from the outside world telling us to stop proclaiming the message of Jesus and internal, the devil wooing us through the world challenging our faith, offering fame and fortune, happiness through things. The believers speak the Word of God, they pray and are empowered by the Holy Spirit to speak boldly. That is how we too answer the external and internal attacks through the Word of God and prayer. It reminds us of the description of ALL IN living earlier in Acts 2:42,

"They devoted themselves to the apostles' teaching and to fellowship, to the breaking of bread and to prayer." Yes, this is where they gained their power and ability to live ALL IN. This focus on the Lord and loving Him with their entire being is what gave them the power to love each other by selling their possessions sharing all that they had.

> Psalm 37:3:5 says, Trust in the Lord and do good. Then you will live safely in the land and prosper. Take delight in the Lord, and he will give you your heart's desires. Commit everything you do to the Lord. Trust him, and he will help you.

Are you holding back and not going ALL IN in your walk with the Lord?

Is God asking you to give Him complete control over the way you spend your time? Your treasures, and talents? What about your work? Perhaps it is your relationships. Is God asking you to commit to Him fully and to entrust your family and relationships to his care? Where might Satan be lying to you and telling you to hold on and keep back instead of giving it all to the Lord?

We can live ALL IN, just as the early church. We have the same tools available; we need to commit fully to Him, all the time, in all areas of life.

Parable of the ducks

The great philosopher Søren Kierkegaard told a story about ducks that came from an imaginary country where only ducks live. One Sunday morning, all the mother and father ducks headed to church with their children waddling behind them. They entered the doors and sat in their duck pews, sang songs from their duck hymnals, and gave to underprivileged ducks at the offering time. When the duck preacher got up to proclaim the message, he was very dynamic. He opened his duck Bible and screamed, "Ducks, you can fly! You have wings and you can fly like eagles." The ducks all chanted, "We can fly, we can fly!" He asked, "Do you believe you can fly?" Again, they shouted back, "We can fly, we can fly." He screamed again, "We can soar through the skies!" They all shouted, "Amen." With that, the pastor closed his duck Bible and dismissed his congregation of ducks. Then they all waddled back home.[12]

So often we hear the Word of God and how His followers are bold and powerful and that through our commitment to Him by the power of the Holy Spirit, we should change our worlds. Living ALL IN is genuinely an all the time commitment. It involves every area of our lives. I challenge you to commit to going ALL IN for the Lord.

But those who trust in the Lord will find new strength. They will soar high on wings like eagles. They will run and not grow weary. They will walk and not faint. (Isaiah 40:31)

"How great is the love the Father has lavished on us, that we should be called children of God! And that is what we are!" (1 John 3:1)

T.I.M.E. #6

Thy Kingdom Come

Thy Kingdom Come! What do you think about when you say these words? If you're anything like me, I would have to admit that I often say them so quickly and by memory that I don't think much at all. I just say them! But, think about the words again. Thy Kingdom Come. What are we asking of the Lord here? Jesus, let your Kingdom come.

Martin Luther reminds us that God's Kingdom certainly comes without our asking, but we ask that it may also come to us. Luther then explains how God's Kingdom comes: "God's Kingdom comes when our heavenly Father gives us His Holy Spirit so that by His grace we believe His Holy Word and lead godly lives here in time and there in eternity."

The Kingdom of God is about His presence and power – here and now and of course then, in eternity. Our families, communities, and relationships are often in some ways broken, but they can be restored and enriched, strengthened and enhanced when we work for God's reign in our lives. When we ask Thy Kingdom Come, we are asking for nothing less than the presence, power, and reign of God's Spirit to fill us and spill out into our world.

I recently finished a book titled *Good Faith, Being a Christian When Society Thinks You're Irrelevant and Extreme,* written by David Kinnaman (The Barna guy) and Gabe Lyons. It is a fascinating book because it describes essentially this struggle of living and bringing God's Kingdom into our world when so much of the world wants nothing to do with it. Consider this quote from the book:

> The research for *Good Faith* leaves little room for doubt that the world is changing around us, making it harder for people to live faithful lives. There are doubts about who to believe and whether the Bible can be trusted, and these fault lines are sometimes pulling Christians and Churches apart.[13]

The research in this book should not be surprising to any, but *Good Faith* describes their research showing that a majority of Americans pledge allegiance to a "new moral code" as they're describing it.

Six guiding principles describe this moral code:

1. To find yourself, look within yourself.
2. People should not criticize someone else's life choices.
3. To be fulfilled in life, pursue the things you desire most.
4. Enjoying yourself is the highest goal of life.
5. People can believe whatever they want as long as those beliefs don't affect society.
6. Any kind of sexual expression between two consenting adults is fine.

The authors go on: "As a result of this shift, we see laws that endorse the broader culture's replacement of Christian morality with the moral code of self-fulfillment. And according to that moral code, any competing morality – say, a religion – that seeks to constrain someone's pursuit of personal fulfillment must itself be constrained."[14]

Yes, this is the morality of self-fulfillment. Perhaps described by praying MY KINGDOM COME! instead.

But Jesus says that we are to Deny ourselves, Turn from your selfish ways, take up your cross, and follow me. If you try to hang on to your life, you will lose it. But if you give up your life for my sake and for the sake of the Good News, you will save it. And what do you benefit if you gain the whole world but lose your own soul? (Mark 8:34-37)

John 17:16, "They do not belong to this world any more than I do."

Paul states in Romans 12:2, "Do not copy the behavior and customs of this world, but let God transform you into a new person by changing the way you think."

IN THE WORLD, NOT OF THE WORLD. No, our moral code is not about self-fulfillment, but self-denial and sacrifice for others. That is what we mean, at least in part, when we pray Thy Kingdom Come.

Ephesians 5:5 states, "You can be sure that no immoral, impure, or greedy person will inherit the Kingdom of

Christ and of God. For a greedy person is an idolater, worshiping the things of this world."

"One day the Pharisees asked Jesus, "When will the Kingdom of God come?" Jesus replied, "The Kingdom of God can't be detected by visible signs. You won't be able to say, 'Here it is!' or 'It's over there!' For the Kingdom of God is already among you." (Luke 17:20-21)

Jesus is already reigning; He has sent His Holy Spirit and that Holy Spirit is at work in the world.

Thy Kingdom Come! What does that mean for us today? First, John 3:5, Jesus answered, "I tell you the truth, no one can enter the Kingdom of God unless he is born of water and the Spirit." It all begins with faith; the faith the God creates in us by His Word and through our baptisms, we are called the People of God.

Second, by our "status" or our NAME, we have a mission. We bring the presence of God wherever we go. When we pray Thy Kingdom Come! We are not passive recipients, although we do receive the power and presence of the Holy Spirit; but, we are then privileged to serve as Jesus

135

served. Mark 10:44-45, "And whoever wants to be a leader among you must be your servant, and whoever wants to be first among you must be the slave of everyone else. For the Son of Man came not to be served but to serve others and to give His life as a ransom for many."

1 Peter 2:12, "Be careful to live properly among your unbelieving neighbors. Then even if they accuse you of doing wrong, they will see your honorable behavior, and they will give honor to God when He judges the world."

. When we pray Thy Kingdom Come, we are asking, at least in part, for the Holy Spirit to work in and through us as we engage the world for the sake of the Gospel. Jesus uses us; He works through the Church and us to bring the Kingdom here.

In 2010, a University of Pennsylvania professor and a nonreligious research group in Philadelphia tried to determine the economic effect of a house of worship on the surrounding community. They wanted to figure out a congregation's financial worth, if any, to the local community it served.

54 different factors were used in their study of ten Protestant churches, one Catholic, and one Jewish Synagogue in Philadelphia. Are you curious…the grand total for the twelve congregations combined? Over 50 million dollars every year!![15] INCREDIBLE!! There is no doubt that our churches provide so much good – bringing the Kingdom of God to the world – in various ways. Of course, working for the Common Good is essential as we work to make this world a better place and this work often permits us to speak the truth of the Reign of Jesus as Lord and Savior of the world. We must be bold in sharing the Truth and the Hope that is in us. Jesus is Lord and His Kingdom is here and He will fully establish it in His timing.

> 1 Corinthians 15:23-27: But there is an order to this resurrection: Christ was raised first; then when comes back, all His people will be raised. After that the end will come, when he turns the Kingdom over to God the Father, having put down all enemies of every kind. For Christ must reign until He humbles all His enemies beneath His feet. And the last enemy to be destroyed is death. For

the Scriptures say, "God has given Him authority over all things.

Does Jesus have authority over all things in your life? We pray "Our Father in Heaven," acknowledging who He is and the relationship we have. Committing to living under His authority carrying His name into the world; acting as His ambassadors. Praying for His Kingdom to come and for His reign over all the earth. What a fantastic and exciting ADVENTURE!! The book of Hebrews concludes with our marching orders, the manner in which we should live in His Kingdom under His reign:

> Since we are receiving a Kingdom that cannot be destroyed, let us be thankful and please God by worshiping Him with holy fear and awe. For our, God is a consuming fire. Continue to love each other with true Christian love. Don't forget to show hospitality to strangers, for some who have done this have entertained angels without realizing it! Don't forget about those in prison. Suffer with them as though you were there yourself. Share the sorrow of those being mistreated, as though you feel their pain in your own bodies.

Give honor to marriage, and remain faithful to one another in marriage. God will surely judge people who are immoral and those who commit adultery. Stay away from the love of money; be satisfied with what you have. For God has said, I will never fail you. I will never forsake you. That is why we can say with confidence, The Lord is my helper, so I will not be afraid. What can mere mortals do to me? (Hebrews 12:28-13:6 NIV)

T.I.M.E. #7

Eyes on the Prize

I don't know if you've ever been to a cross country race before, but I would have to say that it is one of the greatest spectator sports because spectators are genuine participants as well. It is great-fun to watch and follow the pack of coaches, parents, and competitors to different parts of the race course, usually a golf course to cheer on the runners. The runners run by amidst the cheers and screams; there are even school flags and a sign or two urging on the runners. And after the group passes, there's a mad rush to another section to repeat the process again. I suppose it is like spectating for golf, but in fast motion. Run here, run there, yell and scream, certainly no golf clapping.

All of these runners have their "Eyes on the Prize" so to speak. Each of the several hundred runners has a goal for the race. They have to; I know that some have higher expectations than others, there are those who are going to be battling for a win, some are hoping for a personal best, the fastest time of completing the race, and still, others are

141

hoping to finish the race.

The race is an excellent metaphor for our lives, isn't it? Some appear to have the world by the tail, winning at everything they attempt, some become injured, still others are hoping to better themselves, achieve greater things, many are just trying to make it through the day, survive. It is the perfect metaphor for our faith journeys and the Apostle Paul uses it when describing our walk of faith.

> In 1 Corinthians 9:24-25, "Do you not know that in a race all the runners run, but only one gets the prize? Run in such a way as to get the prize. Everyone who competes in the games goes into strict training. They do it to get a crown that will not last, but we do it to get a crown that will last forever."

Sometimes we're afraid to even think about the prize. We know in our heads that eternal life will be fantastic, but it is perhaps somewhat scary to ponder. Fear of the unknown? Maybe, it doesn't even seem to be a prize; instead, the ultimate defeat, death. Keeping our "eyes on the prize" is an excellent way to live, as it reminds us that this earth is not our home and like Paul, we are eagerly awaiting to join Jesus in heaven. Keeping our eyes on the prize helps us run the race.

Let's think about this race called faith. First, we receive faith. The Holy Spirit calls us to faith in Jesus Christ through the Word of God. Through Baptism, we are born again into God's New Covenant. We are children of the Living God.

The race continues as we remain in Jesus. The journey of faith changes us and we are called to walk as Jesus walked. And as we do 2 Corinthians 3:18 tells us, "And we, who with unveiled faces all reflect the Lord's glory, are being transformed into his likeness with ever-increasing glory, which comes from the Lord, who is the Spirit."

We continue the race by remaining in Jesus; we focus on our relationship with Him. Just as the cross country runners train for their races, we too prepare for the race. 1 Timothy 4:8, "For physical training is of some value, but godliness has value for all things, holding promise for both the present life and the life to come." We should be training hard through daily worship, prayer, and reading God's Word and active participation in the life of my church.

Yes! We are in training too. We have our "Eyes on the Prize" as we race through this life. We are part of the New Exodus, as we follow our Moses, the perfect Moses, Jesus to the Promised Land.

It is quite interesting to compare the people of the Old Covenant with those of us living in the New Covenant. Just like the people of God were freed by Him journeying to the Promised Land, following Moses as their Leader; we too are set free, from our bondage to sin, to follow Jesus to the Promised Land, Eternal Life with Him.

The Passover meal with the sacrificial lamb marked the beginning of the journey and the people were commanded to repeat this meal every year to remember the Lord God's deliverance from slavery. The Lord guided them on their journey with his presence through the cloud and pillar of fire. They were brought safely through the Red Sea and the Jordan River as they entered the Promised Land.

We too celebrate a Passover Meal, although Jesus Himself is the Passover Lamb who takes away the sins of the world. The Lord's presence guides us through the Holy Spirit working in us. We too are reborn through the waters of Baptism as we journey, follow the Lord to our Promised Land. The similarities are striking aren't they when we compare the Exodus with the New Exodus?

Where are our "Eyes on the Prize" living? We hardly speak of it. Death is the enemy, but why do we live as though death wins? Sometimes people talk of eternal life as if it is part of our retirement plan, a sort of plan B; well when I leave this playground, I want to have someplace to go that is at least better than hell. Maybe that's why our training lacks gusto sometimes; perhaps we need to take a better look at the prize and what it means for us today.

Hebrews 9:27 states that "it is appointed for mortals to die once and after that face the judgment." Romans 8:10 tells us that our body is dead because of sin. Sin was the direct result of turning away from the Lord God's ways and commands (see also Genesis 2:15-17, Ezekiel 18:4 Note: In T.I.M.E. #14 you will see additional Biblical references that you may choose to look up to further your understanding.   This is also preparation for the final section of the book that follows, which contains many references.) Since all people are born into sin, everyone must die (Psalm 51:5, Romans 3:23, Romans 5:12).

Revelation tells us of the good news The Prize, "and from Jesus Christ, the faithful witness, the firstborn of the dead, and the ruler of the kings of the earth. To him who loves us and freed us from our sins by his blood, and made us to be a kingdom, priests serving his God and Father, to him be glory and dominion forever and ever.   Amen." (Revelation 1:5-6)

We know this, don't we? We know that we are to die once. I pray that you have received Jesus and know where you will spend eternity.

Paul's words in Philippians always help me to refocus on the prize and its importance,

> Not that I have already obtained all this, or have already been made perfect, but I press on to take hold of that for which Christ Jesus took hold of me. Brothers, I do not consider myself yet to have

146

taken hold of it. But one thing I do: Forgetting what is behind and straining toward what is ahead, I press on toward the goal to win the prize for which God has called me heavenward in Christ Jesus. (Philippians 3:12-14 NIV)

It sounds like Paul is giving it his all. How many of us work that hard for the prize? We do not earn the prize, Paul doesn't say that, and he knows that, but still he is working as if he is. I don't think he feels compelled at all or is operating out of a sense of duty; no, I believe he honestly can't wait, he knows the prize is fabulous! Eternal life with Jesus!

Maybe we just haven't spent enough time talking about the prize. For some, just getting through the week is a chore. Race, prize, Lord, please just get me through the week. Perhaps some are leading the pack right now and seemingly do not have any need for God in their life. Hey, things couldn't get much better. We know that our gifts and blessings are to be used for others. We should be helping, walking beside those who are struggling in the race. We're not trying to beat each other in this race; we're trying to get the prize together.

The Century Cross country team that both of my boys have been on forms a shoot/tunnel at the finish line to cheer and bring in each runner until the final one reaches the finish line, the prize. It is pretty cool and I fondly remember standing near other parents enjoying these scenes. On one such an occasion, as the final runner came in, you could see him begin to smile and pick up speed as he anticipated joining his teammates. One mom almost started crying and she said, "I love those boys." It was a grand celebration as they congratulated each other for reaching the goal. The prize. I like to think this is how it will be for us when we receive the prize. A grand celebration!

And what a prize it will be!!

All believers will share in this eternal life of which, Jesus is the firstborn (see 1 Corinthians 15:20, John 11:25-26, John 14:19). There is evidence in the Scriptures that immediately upon death, believers join Jesus until the time of His second coming (see Luke 23:43, Acts 7:59, Philippians 1:23-24, Revelation 19:13).

Jesus told the criminal executed beside him that today he would be with him in paradise (Luke. 23:43) and Paul states that he desires to depart and be with the Lord (Philippians 1:23), which both indicate an immediate joining Jesus upon death. Our bodies remain dead, planted as a seed in the ground.

Finally, Jesus will come surrounded by his angels (see Matthew 16:27, 2 Thessalonians 1:7, Jude 14) and a resurrection of the dead will take place and Jesus will judge both the living and the dead.

Jesus' death and resurrection defeated sin, death, and Satan (see Mark. 8:31, Romans 6:9, Hebrews 2:14). Jesus said that those who believe in him would share in the resurrection (John 11:25-26).

Further, those who receive salvation from Jesus will be raised with a new body to spend eternity with Him (see Job 19:25-27, John. 5:28-29, 1 Corinthians 15:20-57, 1 Thessalonians 4:16). The holy city, the New Jerusalem will come down from heaven and God will make His home among the people (Revelation 21:2-3). "Then he said to me, 'It is done! I am the Alpha and Omega, the beginning and the end. To the thirsty, I will give water as a gift from the spring of the water of life. Those who conquer will inherit these things, and I will be their God and they will be my children'" (Revelation 6-7).

The Scriptures tell this story of love, which is still being fulfilled until Jesus returns with the New Jerusalem when the Lord God will again live among the people and we will be His people he will be our God (Revelation 21). That is the prize we're running for!

T.I.M.E. # 8

God Shows No Partiality

A few years ago I took my boys to an event called, Cowboy Mounted Shooting. It is pretty cool, kind of reenactment of the old west days with horse and rider riding through an obstacle course guns a blazing. The object is to complete the course as fast as possible while also shooting the balloons that are in various positions throughout the course.

Well, I have to admit that it was pretty exciting to watch all of this unfold and I think I might have found my next hobby. One thing that struck me though, upon arrival at the arena, was that we didn't belong. I mean we certainly didn't bring our guns and horses. We had not dressed appropriately, and we didn't speak the language. I mean I know what a single action 45 caliber pistol is, but what is a 6-stage shoot?

We were complete outsiders. I don't think anybody spoke to us that day, most just offered seemingly uncomfortable smiles, as if to say, "the city is back that way."

This makes me think about a story from the Bible. Peter and Cornelius were worlds apart. Jew and Gentile. These two groups just didn't hang out together. Remember, Cornelius was a God-fearer. He was a centurion in the Italian Regiment, regularly giving to those in need and he prayed to God regularly. Apparently, he did not know Jesus yet as Jesus' message would move from Jerusalem to Judea then to the ends of the earth. We see that movement in the book of Acts in Scripture. So, an angel of the Lord told Cornelius to send for Peter. It just so happened that Peter would also receive a visit from the Lord. Peter though, would need more convincing because he was a devout Jew. Jews didn't socialize with the Gentiles. The Holy Spirit would make an incredible statement regarding the People of God through this story sometimes called "The Gentile Pentecost." Those present were going to learn that God does not play favorites, He shows no partiality when it comes to the offer of His Grace. We pick up the story after Cornelius was told to send for Peter and Peter was shown through his vision that indeed God shows no favorites. Acts 10:34-36,

Then Peter began to speak: "I now realize how

true it is that God does not show favoritism but accepts men from every nation who fear him and do what is right. You know the message God sent to the people of Israel, telling the good news of peace through Jesus Christ, who is Lord of all." (NIV)

First of all, this is a huge statement! The people of Israel were God's chosen. To think of God in terms of every nation would be a rather significant paradigm shift. God's favor is available for all people! What this is not saying though, is that all people are IN as in Universalism, which is so popular and present in our culture. Not, "all roads lead to God," but that all people stand equally before God. We are all condemned sinners, we all need Jesus. Doing right as described here is not "works righteousness," or earning one's salvation, but fearing the Lord and placing one's faith in Him. It is more accurately stating that Jesus is the only way to salvation, but this gift of Grace through Faith is available to everyone, not just Israel.

"You know what has happened throughout Judea, beginning in Galilee after the baptism that John preached— how God anointed Jesus of Nazareth with the Holy Spirit and power, and how he went around doing good and healing all who were under the power of the devil because God was with him. We are witnesses of everything he did in the country of the Jews and in Jerusalem. They killed him by hanging him on a tree, but God raised him from the dead on the third day and caused him to be seen. He was not seen by all the people, but by witnesses whom God had already chosen—by us who ate and drank with him after he rose from the dead. He commanded us to preach to the people and to testify that he is the one whom God appointed as judge of the living and the dead. All the prophets testify about him that everyone who believes in him receives forgiveness of sins through his name." (Acts 10:37-43 NIV)

Peter begins to tell the message of Jesus and offers a reasonably comprehensive review. It is interesting, but not surprising that Peter does not quote Scripture when talking about Jesus here. He merely tells the story to those who probably did not know the Jewish Scriptures. He does tell the story, as one with the command of an eyewitness, also by the power of the Holy Spirit. He had spent three years with, learned from, seen the risen Jesus and was now proclaiming His authority. Jesus is King and His healing and doing good is tied to the battle present in creation. Christ's power overcomes the devil and his forces, which seek to destroy humanity. He had demonstrated this in his actions of the previous years; he ultimately proved it by conquering death. Peter witnessed all of it.

> While Peter was still speaking these words, the Holy Spirit came on all who heard the message. The circumcised believers who had come with Peter were astonished that the gift of the Holy Spirit had been poured out even on the Gentiles. "For they heard them speaking in tongues and praising God." Then Peter said, "Can anyone keep these people from being baptized with water? They have received the Holy Spirit just as we have." So he ordered that they be baptized in the name of Jesus Christ. Then they asked Peter to stay with them for a few days. (Acts 10:44-48 NIV)

Wow, the Holy Spirit interrupted Peter's sermon! What an awesome occurrence. The Jewish Christians were astonished. They thought the promise of the Holy Spirit was limited to Israel. Yet, the Holy Spirit came upon the Gentiles just as it had the Jews, remember Acts 2? This sounds very similar, doesn't it? Faith had come to them just as it did in Acts 2; they received New Covenant power and the fullness of the Holy Spirit. They were accepted by God not for following the Mosaic Law but received the Holy Spirit by believing, through their faith in Jesus as the one who forgives sins.

Now, we could quickly get into a discussion on baptism here. This might seem to fit with those who believe baptism is merely an outward sign of an inward faith. It seems that could be the case here. I think what is important is that Peter ordered them to be baptized. That would seem to make it much more than a simple outward sign. Remember, Peter later writes in a letter that baptism now saves you (1 Peter 3:19). I believe we are safe in declaring that it is more than symbolism, but a sacred act commanded by the Lord.

The Lord takes over here by interrupting with at least the fourth outpouring of the Holy Spirit presented in the book of Acts. Peter compares it to the first. The circumcised believers were not expecting this. God does not play favorites. The key to receiving forgiveness is by believing the testimony of the prophets and later prophetic figures like Peter, the eyewitnesses, so obtaining the release from sins through Jesus' name. This is truly incredible!

This is a fantastic story of conversions. Not only people believing in Jesus and the establishment of His Kingdom but also a newfound belief in who constitutes the People of God. Many Gentiles learned and believed "that everyone who believes in him receives forgiveness of sins through his name." But, let's not miss the other very important conversion here. Peter and the other circumcised believers also learned who the true church was. A new community was formed. Jew and Gentile are the People of God and they were to interact freely. Not only were people being reconciled to God, but there is also reconciliation between Jew and Gentile.

There is so much here to think about isn't there? It struck me while preparing this message that I could learn so much from Peter, how about you? We have an evangelical speech offered by Peter to persuade any and all who were listening that Jesus is the Christ, the Son of God, sent into the world to redeem people, to save them from their sins and restore a proper relationship with the living God. I need the reminder of that promise today. It's so awesome to be forgiven, isn't it?

Perhaps, the not so great part for me anyway, is that this message IS for everyone. I get a little uncomfortable when I think about reaching out to those who are not "my kind." I think about my bit of uneasiness at the Cowboy Mounted Shooting event and I wonder how many people feel that way in our churches-if they dare walk in. How many people will not even consider a church because they know they will not fit in? When I read this passage of Scripture, I am convicted and think, "Where is my burden for the lost?" It is very troubling. Indeed, my first thought in viewing those who are different than me, those who don't share my beliefs, those who look different than me, you know, those people; is not usually a passion and burden for them to know the Lord. I believe this message is supposed to create and convict all of us in this.

Not too long ago I was at a dinner function with my wife. There were many bright, educated and some quite sophisticated people present. I felt somewhat out of place and even a bit uncomfortable. One of the men approached me and struck up some small talk, which very quickly led to, what do you do? It's always quite interesting to observe the reaction when people learn that I am a pastor. Many times people seem to feel the need of telling why they either do not attend church anymore or why they have a problem with Christianity. On this particular occasion, the gentleman wanted to have a theological discussion of sorts on the authority of Scripture. Primarily, the discussion went to the Bible's view on a couple of social issues.

Well, at the time, I felt quite proud of myself for declaring by using Scripture how my view was correct. On these particular issues, if one holds to the authority of Scripture as the inspired Word of God there are no gray areas. I am still convinced of that. I wonder where my heart was/is though. I was and sometimes am more concerned about being right than I am about my burden for the other person. I never did get a chance to ask this gentleman what his thoughts were regarding the Lord Jesus or if he placed his faith in Him. No, I had won the argument and moved on to lighter topics, "think the Twins will win tomorrow?"

I hope and pray that this message will move us all to action. I hope and pray that this message will increase/give us a burden for those who do not know Jesus. I hope and pray that our eyes will be opened as Peter's were to the inclusiveness of the Gospel. I love how John says the same thing in 1 John chapter 1:3-4

> We proclaim to you what we have seen and heard, so that you also may have fellowship with us. And our fellowship is with the Father and with his Son, Jesus Christ. We write this to make our joy complete.

Not only do we share in this incredible gift of grace, but we also experience joy as others join in the fellowship. Amazing! "Truly I understand that God shows no partiality, but in every nation anyone who fears him and..."

T.I.M.E. #9

Our Father

Have you heard the name, Richard Dawkins? Do you know who he is? He has been described as the driver of the atheist bus and is undoubtedly one of the most outspoken atheists in the world. On June 9th, 2015, he visited Rochester, MN. Opening comments from the evening, "We are going to have an evening of a little bit of science, a little bit of blasphemy, and a little bit of fun. I had the good fortune of not being brought up Catholic…I was brought up with the "weak tea" version, the Anglican version of faith. My parents were not religious, but I was sent to Anglican school. Chapel and prayers every day read Scripture, etc. But, it wasn't thrust down our throats, not indoctrination. I eventually realized it was nonsense; however, I was left thinking there must be something-deist belief perhaps, because of the beauty of life, the elegance of life – I studied biology. Then I finally understood Darwin, I suppose, that there was now no reason whatsoever to believe and then I became an Atheist."

Dawkins is leading a charge of "New Atheism" as it is being called, that is becoming more and more aggressive.

Yes, Dawkins claims that 9/11 radicalized him. Listen to this statement by Dawkins:

> My last vestige of "hands-off religion" respect disappeared in the smoke and choking dust of September 11, 2001, followed by the "
> 'National Day of Prayer", when prelates and pastors did their tremulous Martin Luther King impersonation and urged people of mutually incompatible faiths to hold hands, united in homage to the very force that caused the problem in the first place.

WOW!!

So, since religion is the problem, according to the New Atheists, then it is rather simple. Get rid of religion.

The sad reality is that this kind of thinking is growing and gaining ground. Although the actual statistics and number of those who are atheist are debated; we know that the "churchless" population is growing as well as those who claim "none" as a religious affiliation. It is sad. It is a call and an opportunity for Christians to witnesses; to shine

162

God's light and love in the world. It truly begins in our own homes. We know the battle is in our schools, our work, and our community who would invite Richard Dawkins to enlighten us.

The Lord's Prayer, the prayer that Jesus taught His followers to pray contains the answer to a defense of new atheism and any misguided thinking. It is an offensive and defensive weapon, but the Lord's prayer also contains answers; responses to the many questions and challenges that the new atheists present. I suppose those are bold claims, but they are reliable and secure claims to be sure! Would we expect any less from a model prayer given to us by Jesus?

> "Our Father who art in heaven." With these words, God tenderly invites us to believe that He is our true Father and that we are His true children, so that with all boldness and confidence we may ask Him as dear children ask their beloved father. (Luther's Small Catechism)

I find it interesting that the Apostles' Creed begins with similar words: "I believe in God the Father Almighty,

Maker of Heaven and Earth." Essentially, Jesus is calling us to begin the Lord's Prayer, to begin any prayer in this manner, saying the same. Psalm 124:8, "Our help is in the name of the Lord, who made heaven and earth." Just like the Scriptures, our confession and our faith are built from the Creation – the beginning. Isn't it an exciting posture that Jesus tells us, in which to begin prayer?

I find Richard Dawkins' comments about the beauty and elegance of Life very interesting. As a scientist, he acknowledges the incredible nature of the creation. And yet, he accepts evolution as the answer for creation. Even within the scientific community, the theory of evolution is crumbling. David Berlinski, a scholar from Princeton and Scientist, who openly claims to be a skeptic, an agnostic perhaps writes:

> The effort by Darwinian biologists to promote Darwin is simply explained. Within the English-speaking world, Darwin's theory of evolution remains the only scientific theory to be widely championed by the scientific community and widely disbelieved by everyone else. No matter the effort made by biologists, the thing continues

to elicit the same reaction it has always elicited: You've got to be kidding, right? There is wide appreciation of the fact that if biologists are wrong about Darwin, they are wrong about life, and if they are wrong about life, they are wrong about everything.[16]

These are not the words of a committed follower of Jesus, merely the words of a scientific skeptic! WHY?

The Apostle Paul states, "For what can be known about God is plain to them because God has shown it to them. For His invisible attributes, namely, his eternal power and divine nature have been clearly perceived, ever since the creation of the world, in the things that have been made. So they are without excuse. (Romans 1:19-20).

The fool says in his heart, "There is no God." (Psalm 14:1)

When we pray Our Father who art in heaven, we are acknowledging who He is; He is the creator of the heavens and the earth. We are humbling ourselves before the Mighty Presence of the Lord! It all begins here!

Acts 17:24, "The God who made the world and everything in it is Lord of Heaven and Earth."

This is our starting point: How do you see God? When we pray, "Our Father who art in Heaven;" it should put us in a position of humility, as we acknowledge who He is and who we are before Him.

Now, we can move to the perhaps more fantastic part of this incredible statement; at least more incredible for you and me. We are called to pray "OUR FATHER"! This amazing Creator God!! Jesus says God is Our Father!! When we think about people in Jesus' day daring to address God as Father, it shows even more so, how incredible it is for Jesus to say this. People at this time didn't even risk saying the word for God – YAHWEH out loud for fearing of taking God's name in vain.

But to Jesus and as He shows us; God is not a distant God. No, He is loving and desires a relationship with us. The

Lord God is as a loving Parent. 1 John 3:1, "See what kind of love the Father has given us, that we should be called children of God; and so we are. The reason why the world does not know us is that it did not know Him."

Incredible!! How is this possible one may ask? "For in Christ Jesus, you are all sons of God, through faith." Yes, it is through faith created in us by the power of the Holy Spirit, where we can walk intimately with Our Father." (Galatians 3:26 NIV)

Yes, Romans 8:15-16, "You have received the Spirit of adoption as sons…The Spirit Himself bears witness with our spirit that we are children of God." (NIV)

That is the Good News!! The Almighty God, Creator of the universe, Creator of You and Me; desires a relationship with every one of us!! Think about that as you begin a prayer to Him. Think about the words, Our Father who art in heaven, as you witness to others. The Holy Spirit works in mysterious ways through the Word of God.

And God has given us His Spirit (not the world's spirit), so we can know the beautiful things God has freely given us. When we tell you this, we do not use words of human wisdom. We speak words given to us by the Spirit, using the Spirit's words to explain spiritual truths…we who have the Spirit understand these things, but others can't understand us at all. How could they? For, Who can know what the Lord is thinking? Who can give Him counsel? But we can understand these things, for we have the mind of Christ. (1 Corinthians 2:12-16 NLT)

T.I.M.E. #10
Are you capable?

"If you plan on being anything less than you are capable of being you will probably be unhappy all the days of your life." Abraham Maslow

That's a great quote, isn't it? Do you remember Maslow? Hierarchy of needs, psychology classes? Do you think it's true?

The Scriptures say:
"God yearns jealously for the spirit that he has made to dwell in us." (James 4:5)

Placing anything before God and our relationship with Him is "Being less than we are capable of being." I wonder how many people would look at us Christians and describe our lives as happy and fulfilled? Living lives of joy?

Walk into any bookstore, and you will find walls of books about personal improvement, enlightenment, pop-psychology, self-help, meditation, Eastern religions, and many on the ever-popular subject of spirituality. So many people are searching today, searching for happiness, joy, The Truth.

They try to find it by looking within themselves. Too many try to find meaning and purpose in the very things that will only continue to let them down: pleasure or possessions. We are constantly tempted to look for truth in the wrong places. What then is the truth? How can one find contentment, joy, peace, happiness; how can you be all that you are capable of being? How may it be found in the world today?

Jesus said, "For this, I was born, and for this I have come into the world, to bear witness to the truth. Everyone on the side of truth listens to me." (John 18:37)

"The promise we are standing on today comes from very familiar words of Jesus: 'I am the way and the truth and the life. No one comes to the Father except through me.'" John 14:6

Many people, even many who do not follow Jesus, can recite these words. We live in a pluralistic culture. Our neighbors, co-workers, and friends come from many different religious backgrounds. They seem just as moral and religious as we are, if not more so. All of them promising a path to "Being all we are capable of being." It seems the height of arrogance to think that we Christians alone have the right religion and that everyone else is lost forever.

We also live in a climate of relativism. Because of our pluralism and the dominating worldview of postmodernism, people tend to assume that truth, morality, and religion are relative. According to this way of thinking, cultures and individuals construct ways of thinking and acting that give meaning to their lives, but meaning is strictly subjective. There is no objective truth—with perhaps the exception of scientifically determined facts—that is valid for everyone.

Sadly, when believer states Jesus' promise in John 14:6, it is too often exclaimed with an almost defiant and happy winning ending in an argument. "JESUS SAID I AM THE WAY..."!! I WIN!! Enough said!! That is not the way Jesus delivered the words.

If we look at Jesus' words more closely and the entire book of John, we realize that Jesus is not happily delivering an ultimatum. He is NOT saying, choose me, and that's it; if you don't pick me, I'm going to get you, I'm going to condemn you to live apart from me in eternity. No!!

In John 12:47, Jesus said, "As for the person who hears my words but does not keep them, I do not judge him. For I did not come to judge the world, but to save it."

Jesus is saying; I am the way, I have come for you out of love for you. I am the ONLY way because I am the only one who has the credentials to pull this mission off. It is not choose me or else; it is I AM YOUR ONLY HOPE! In fact, it is only through me where you will be able to "Be all that you are capable of being."

> Hebrews 2:14-18 (NLT):
> Because God's children are human beings – made of flesh and blood – the Son also became flesh and blood. For only as a human being could he die, and only by dying could he break the power of the devil, who had the power of death. Only in this

way could he set free all who have lived their lives as slaves to the fear of dying.

We also know that the Son did not come to help angels; he came to help the descendants of Abraham. Therefore, it was necessary for him to be made in every respect like us, his brothers and sisters, so that he could be our merciful and faithful High Priest before God. Then he could offer a sacrifice that would take away the sins of the people. Since he himself has gone through suffering and testing, he is able to help us when we are being tested.

In John 13, Jesus had delivered some troubling news to his disciples, telling them they could not go where He was going. He had spoken of these things already, but the disciples didn't understand all that was going on. Now, it is time. It is all going to become very real. Jesus must continue the mission on his own. As we learned in Hebrews, and of course in many places in Scriptures, only Jesus can complete the mission. He is uniquely qualified. He is the Son of God. The disciples, of course, want to go too. Especially, Peter, "I will lay down my life for you

Lord." Interestingly, Jesus tells Peter that he will even deny that he knows Jesus.

Can you imagine their concern? No wonder Jesus tells them not to let their hearts be troubled. Troubled was probably an understatement! "Lord, help us. Show us the way." Don't leave us!" Here is the place, the Lord is calling all people by His Word, by the power of the Holy Spirit to the place where they realize that they cannot go it alone.

Jesus calls all people to follow Him, to place their complete faith and trust in Him so that they can live to be all they are created to be. To live life, THE FULL LIFE, in Him by the power of the Holy Spirit living out the mission that He began that continues through His followers.

Jesus answered, "I am the way and the truth and the life. No one comes to the Father except through me." (John 14:6).

Are you "Being anything less than you are capable of being" today? Is your heart troubled today? Is God's spirit within you yearning jealously today? Here's the call to action.

John 14:11, Jesus says, "Just believe that I am in the Father and the Father is in me. Or at least believe because of the work you have seen me do." The entire book of John is written so that we may believe. John 20:30-31,

The disciples saw Jesus do many other miraculous signs in addition to the ones recorded in this book. But these are written so that you may continue to believe that Jesus is the Messiah, the Son of God and that by believing in him you will have life by the power of his name. (NLT)

Living to be all we are capable of being, includes living out John 14:6, I am the way, the truth, and the life. Jesus is the way, calling us to faith and complete trust in him and also living as He lived, as He commanded us to live.

After washing the disciple's feet, Jesus said he had given them, given us an example to follow. Serve others. John 12:34, "So now I am giving you a new commandment: Love each other. Just as I have loved you, you should love each other."

Yes, once we believe, once we're on the path of THE WAY, it's not over. We're called to live a certain way, imitating Jesus in the world. That's hard, isn't it? Think back to the image of that bookstore with all of the options, all of "the ways" competing for our attention, all "the ways" telling us how to live. It's okay though, we move on in faith and trust, believing and although we cannot explain it, other than declaring Jesus' promise "

> If you love me, you will keep my commandments. And I will ask the Father, and he will give you another Advocate, to be with you forever. This is the Spirit of truth, whom the world cannot receive because it neither sees him nor knows him. You know him because he abides with you, and he will be in you. (John 14:15-17)

T.I.M.E. # 11

God's Will

Your will be done on earth as it is in heaven.

–The Lord's Prayer

Do you remember this one: Two all beef patty, special sauce, lettuce, cheese, pickles, onions, on a sesame seed bun. YES, McDonald's Big Mac. I remember those commercials specifically in the mid-1970s. And then, of course, the Rival: Have it your way, Have it your way, have it your way at Burger King. Hold the pickles, hold the lettuce, special orders, don't upset us. All we ask is that you let us serve it your way. Have it your way!! Now that' the way to do it, my way!!

Yes, some of us remember those, don't we? In some ways, this little "burger war" is a metaphor for the significant shift that is occurring in our country isn't it? More and more we want it my way. It's all about the individual – ME!

177

English author Aldous Huxley is famous for saying, "The third petition of the Lord's Prayer is repeated daily by millions who have not the slightest intention of letting anyone's will be done but their own."

It would be hard to argue against our country being a "Have it your way" nation, wouldn't it? Of course, there is a shift in our country, and there is no doubt we see moral decay, but it would be a mistake for us to think that this is unique to our day. People have been selfish since The Fall of humankind recorded in Genesis chapter 3 of the Bible. Thankfully, "The good and gracious will of God is done even without our prayers, but we pray in this petition that it may be done among us also."

Martin Luther writes in the Large Catechism, "No one can believe how the devil opposes and resists these prayers. He cannot allow anyone to teach or to believe rightly. It hurts him beyond measure to have his lies and abominations exposed...So he provokes the world against us, fans and stirs the fire, so that he may hinder and drive us back, cause us to fall, and again bring us under his power."

1 Peter 5:8, "Be self-controlled and alert. Your enemy, the devil, prowls around like a roaring lion looking for someone to devour." "

"Such is all his will, mind, and thought. He strives for this day and night and never rests a moment." -Luther

We know life is a struggle and we struggle against selfish desires and living the ways of the world, which is under the control of the devil. We follow Jesus' example, "Going a little farther, He fell with His face to the ground and prayed, 'My Father, if it is possible, may this cup be taken from me. Yet not as I will, but as you will." (Luke 22) Yes, we must surrender our will to God's. Is there some area of your life that is not surrendered to the Lordship of Jesus?

Luther writes in the Small Catechism, "God's will is done when He breaks and hinders every evil plan and purpose of the devil, the world, and our sinful nature, which do not want us to hallow God's name or let His kingdom come; and when He strengthens and keeps us firm in His Word and faith until we die. This is His good and gracious will."

Yes, He helps us in our battles and struggles:

> 2 Corinthians 12:9-10, But he said to me, "My grace is sufficient for you, for my power is made perfect in weakness." Therefore I will boast all the more gladly of my weaknesses, so that the power of Christ may rest upon me. For the sake of Christ, then, I am content with weaknesses, insults, hardships, persecutions, and calamities. For when I am weak, then I am strong.

2 Corinthians 4:8-9, "We are afflicted in every way, but not crushed; perplexed, but not driven to despair; persecuted, but not forsaken; struck down, but not destroyed;"

Joshua 1:9, "Have I not commanded you? Be strong and courageous. Do not be frightened, and do not be dismayed, for the LORD your God is with you wherever you go."

1 Corinthians 10:13, "No temptation has overtaken you that is not common to man. God is faithful, and He will not let you be tempted beyond your ability, but with the temptation, He will also provide the way of escape, that you may be able to endure it."

Yet, not as I will, but as you will Lord!

Jesus said in John 6:40, "For my Father's will is that everyone who looks to the Son and believes in Him shall have eternal life, and I will raise him up at the last day."

Romans 12:2, "Do not conform any longer to the pattern of this world, but be transformed by the renewing of your mind. Then you will be able to test and approve what God's will is – His good, pleasing, and perfect will."

God helps us in our struggle. His Holy Spirit empowers us and strengthens us, keeps us in the faith. Jesus taught us, and we read in the Scriptures that we are in a real battle with Satan and a world system designed to ruin our lives, especially our faith life.

God's will is that we will know Him. That we will know Jesus, His death and resurrection and His offer of Life!! Life in His name through faith and trust in Him. The evil one does NOT want us to live this life of love and faith in our Lord. His world offers so many tempting and appealing distractions that take our eyes off Jesus.

Jesus also showed the way to victory over the world's temptations to be able to live God's will in our lives.

This week I came across an excellent Scriptural model for this very thing. A model for knowing God's will for living life:

You can know God's will for your life. He promises, 'I will instruct you and teach you in the way you should go.' Psalm 32:8 His Word says, 'In all your ways acknowledge Him, and He shall direct your paths' (Proverbs 3:6). God wants you to move from guesswork to guidance, but getting there requires four things:

1) Knowing that God's will begins with surrendering your will. Jesus said, 'I do not seek My own will, but the will of Him who sent Me' (John 5:30). You only recognize God's

will as you learn to lay aside your own will, and that gets easier with practice.

2) Keeping a spiritual mindset. It's not possible to sense God's will while self-interest controls you. 'The mind governed by the flesh is hostile to God. It does not submit to God's law, nor can it do so' (Romans 8:7).

3) Praying for God's guidance. David prayed, 'Teach me to do Your will, for You are my God; may Your good Spirit lead me...' (Psalms 143:10). James also encourages us: 'If you need wisdom, ask our generous God, and He will give it to you. He will not rebuke you for asking' (James 1:5).

4) Reading God's Word with a heart that's open to hearing from Him. 'By your words, I can see where I'm going; they throw a beam of light on my dark path...' (Psalm 119:105 MSG). Daily exposure to the Word of God will help you recognize His voice when He speaks to you. '...The sheep follow Him: for they know His voice' (John 10:4).

Jesus shows us how we're transformed by the renewing of our minds. John 8:31-32, "Jesus was saying to those Jews who had believed Him, 'If you continue in My word, then you are truly disciples of Mine; and you will know the truth, and the truth shall make you free."

We all need to read, study, memorize and meditate on God's Word. Where is the world squeezing you into its mold? Hebrews 12:2, "Let us fix our eyes on Jesus, the author, and perfecter of our faith, who for the joy set before Him endured the cross, scoring its shame, and sat down at the right hand of the throne of God."

We must also not give up meeting together. Hebrews 10:24-25, "Let us think of ways to motivate one another to acts of love and good works. And let us not neglect our meeting together, as some people do, but encourage one another, especially now that the day of his return is drawing near."

Jude 20-21, "But you, dear friends, must build each other up in your most holy faith, pray in the power of the Holy Spirit, and await the mercy of our Lord Jesus Christ, who will bring you eternal life. In this way, you will keep yourselves safe in God's love."

Awesome, be in the Word!! Meet together and build each other up!! Pray always!! Especially, our Lord's Prayer!!

Thy will be done!!
The reality is our minds are like play-do. They are shaped into whatever we let influence them. What is shaping your mind today? Think about all of the distractions...
What in the world do you need to say "no" to?
What in God's Word do you need to say "yes" to?

> Don't store up treasure here on earth, where moths eat them and rust destroys them, and where thieves break in and steal. Store your treasures in heaven, where moths and rust cannot destroy, and thieves do not break in and steal. Wherever your treasure is, there the desires of your heart will be. (Matthew 6:19-21 NIV)

T.I.M.E. # 12

Some Doubted!

When they saw Him, they worshiped him; but some doubted...(Matthew 28:17)
WHAT? SOME DOUBTED!!!

What is that doing in the Bible? Who doubted? How many doubted? Are we talking specifically about some of the 11 disciples? What did they doubt? Were their doubts resolved? MATTHEW DOESN'T SAY.

I don't know about you, but when I read and think about The Great Commission (Matthew 28:16-20), this famous and familiar passage of Scripture, I do not give much thought to this little phrase, "but some doubted." I usually jump right over it. What do we typically dwell on in this passage? GO! Right? I believe it is good to slow down and even pause here.

Isn't it interesting that Matthew leaves us and lets us live with the tension of not knowing if and how their doubts might have been resolved? That's troubling, isn't it? Or is it? It seems to me that the only explanation is that it is true! If Matthew were writing a piece of fiction here why would he include this?

I love this! What better defense of the Gospel? It is merely an objective description of reality. Matthew's focus and purpose for writing are a bit different from say John's who clearly states that he wrote so that you will believe that Jesus is the Messiah, the Son of God.
Matthew is writing to convince the people of Israel that Jesus is the one written about in the prophets. He is the fulfillment of the Old Covenant, the promised one described in Isaiah.

Matthew certainly wants his readers to believe in Jesus; he has a different focus, which ultimately is of great benefit for any to believe.

What a great foundation to build from, a foundation from which to Make Disciples. Perhaps it helps us come to this famous passage a bit differently so that we can listen to what the Lord will teach us.

Imagine the raw emotion that must have been present here.

Familiarity dulls (I believe) our hearing here. Yes, this incredible story of Jesus' resurrection, God raised Jesus from the dead. Amazing. But, think about the people present here! The man they have been following, learning from, seeing that he is different. He is mighty and powerful; he said he is the one. The king who is to come and restore Israel. But, they killed him. Imagine the grief and sorrow of this amazing life cut so short.

Now imagine the confusion, fear, perhaps even terror in recognizing and seeing this Jesus again. I believe it is difficult for us to grab the magnitude of it all. I don't think doubt is used here in the same way that we might use it today. One LCMS scholar said that we do the word translated here as doubt disservice. Forgive me for repeating this, but he stated that the response was more "they filled their pants" than one of doubt. They were scared! Who is this?! HOW CAN THIS BE?

When we consider the force of the Great Commission, Making Disciples, we must start with this question. "Who is this?" This is what Matthew does in his entire book. Matthew roots Jesus the Messiah, in history beginning his book with Jesus' genealogy. Jesus had the bloodlines

Abraham to David, through the Babylonian exile to the Christ, the Savior (Matthew 1:17). Then immediately following in chapter one we read that Jesus was also from the Holy Spirit. Truly the Son of God, Emmanuel – God with us (Matthew 1:23). Incredible!! Born of a virgin united with man.

Matthew writes to show us that the Kingdom of God has arrived in and through Jesus.

The age to come has been launched in Jesus' resurrection. Jesus has come to restore humanity to the Lord God. Making Disciples grows out of this reality.
"But who do you say that I am?" Remember when Jesus asked Peter this in Matthew 16:15? A disciple of Jesus must first answer this question for himself before Making Disciples. We end or is it begin on the mountain with Jesus telling the disciples to go Make Disciples.

Building and working off of the solid foundation of who Jesus is-we go and Make Disciples. WHO DO YOU SAY JESUS IS?

I love that we're on the mountain with Jesus as he gives these instructions. Remember, back in chapter 4 of this Gospel, Satan has taken Jesus to the mountain so to speak and has shown Him all that he would give him if he would worship him. Jesus conquers the devil, and now sin and death and the Lord God has given Him everything, all authority over the heavens and the earth. Here we are standing with Jesus overlooking it all, and He says go, it is all yours.

It is not yours to use for your glory, as the devil might tell us. It is yours to go and Make Disciples. Making Disciples is the main verb here. Not Go as we so often land on. In the original language make disciples is the imperative, the command. The other three-go, baptize and teach are in support or HOW one makes disciples.

First, we do have to go. We've got to leave the mountain; we've got to look beyond "ME" our glory, the selfishness the devil tempts us with and go. Where is God calling you to go and make disciples? It might be in your own family, in your church family or another area of influence in your life. Maybe it is INDIA or some other far off place, it could be all of the above, but clearly, the Lord has given you a burden for making disciples.

Second, is baptism. We follow Jesus' example, as we become part of His Family through baptism. Titus 3:5 and following say "He saved us, not because of righteous things we had done, but because of his mercy. He saved us through the washing of rebirth and renewal by the Holy Spirit, who he poured out on us generously through Jesus Christ our Savior."

We receive the promise of new life, life everlasting with Jesus, Romans 6 "We were therefore buried with Him through baptism into death in order that, just as Christ was raised from the dead through the glory of the Father, we too may live a new life."
The new life...this leads us to our third point in making disciples.

Teaching. How does one live in obedience to all that Jesus has commanded? I suppose we could say that this is impossible. I cannot live like Jesus, I am a sinner. And of course, this is true. However, the last statement gives us our hope and power.

And remember, I am with you always, to the end of the age.

Living in obedience is different than living without sin. Jesus' power and presence help us live in obedience to Him and follow His teaching.

> John 14:26-27, Jesus said; "But the advocate, the Holy Spirit, whom the Father will send in my name, will teach you all things and will remind you of everything I have said to you. Peace I leave with you; my peace I give you. I do not give to you as the world gives. Do not let your hearts be troubled and do not be afraid."

How are you doing in obedience to our Lord?

Here are some questions and a Great Commission to wrestle with today.

Are you making disciples?

Are you listening for your go?

Are you making sure those in your circle of influence are baptized?

Are you keeping your baptismal promises to your children?

Are you teaching others and also yourself to obey Jesus?

Making disciples is a tall order! It is a huge responsibility to be sure. It is not easy. There are and will always be doubters.

"Have no fear! And surely I am with you always, to the very end of the age."

I asked my son Zeke for permission to share this. For one of their classes way back in elementary school, they were asked to write a letter to Bill Nye, the Science Guy in response to a video they had watched in science class titled, "Bill Nye, Creationism is Not Appropriate for Children."

I have not seen the video. What struck me though, in reading the letter that Zeke had written, was not so much the content, but the fact that we're making disciples in our churches and homes.

I could not thank God enough as I read a short letter where Zeke, in the end, shared his hope in the Lord Jesus. Dr. Nye is an atheist and a very intelligent man. One could not win an argument with him in the realm of the physical, science and all of that.

It was truly humbling, inspiring, and impressive to see Zeke land on hope and faith. He sees and understands the importance of placing our faith in the ONE WHO IS WITH US ALWAYS. One cannot measure this; one cannot argue with this, it is beyond yet near every one of us. He gives us the hope and peace that surpasses all understanding.

Let's continue this amazing adventure of MAKING DISCIPLES!

T.I.M.E. # 13

Heaven

Heaven. Do you ever think about it? What do you know and believe about heaven?

The apostle Paul writes in Philippians 1:23, "I desire to depart and be with Christ, which is better by far." Wow, is that how we view our departure from this world?

One of the most frequent questions I received when I was skydiving for a living was, "What do you do if your parachute doesn't open?" The answer is that you open your reserve parachute. The next logical question is…? "Have you ever had to use yours?" Well yes, I have. I have used my reserve parachute two times. The very first time came shortly after I learned a new method of packing the main parachute. A few of us were at an event where we noticed a few people who were very fast at packing parachutes while using a seemingly messy method of straightening lines and quickly folding everything to save time and get back in the air. It was called "trash packing, " and it certainly looked like a garbage bag of trash. So, a couple of us observed and learned how to trash pack.

A few days later we were jumping, and I was in a hurry to make the next load and thought I could save some time and so I did a quick trash pack of my parachute and raced to the airplane. We had a beautiful free fall for a minute or so; then as I opened my parachute things didn't feel right, and I looked up to confirm what I already knew. I had an ugly mess up there with lines twisted...and I was in a violent spin falling fast. I could NOT land this mess. I pulled the cutaway handle releasing the main parachute and went back into freefall where I immediately opened the reserve parachute. Safe!

Sadly, I think this is how many people view heaven. We are free-falling our way through life, perhaps even having a good time enticed by the joys and desires of this world and we think, if we do have a problem, a malfunction, we better have a reserve parachute. Of course, we know that life on this earth is temporary and we better have a backup plan, and heaven is probably better than the alternative, right?

John Eldredge, the author of the men's book, *Wild at Heart* bluntly states that heaven as often described in the church quite frankly sounds boring or like the never-ending church service in the sky. Not too exciting for many. "Floating around on the clouds playing the harp..."

Is that what the Scriptures show us? That heaven is like a reserve parachute, a backup plan, an eternal church service? Not quite as good as the here and now, but certainly better than the alternative? We hear it presented this way at times, don't we? You're a sinner! You better repent so that you can go to heaven when you die. This is most definitely true, and we should desire to live in heaven, but I believe it is so much more than an insurance plan.

What is a proper Biblical view of heaven?

First of all, heaven is not described as a place to go to, as in a geographic location, such as, putting the coordinates into a GPS and driving to Chicago. We are not told that. Heaven or paradise is defined as being with the Lord. The repentant thief on the cross is told by Jesus, "Today you will be with me in paradise." When Stephen is being stoned he says, "Lord Jesus receive my spirit," and as previously mentioned, Paul states, "It is my desire to be with Christ."

Revelation 14:13 says, "Whoever dies in the Lord is blessed from henceforth." It is undoubtedly a place because Jesus states in John 14:1-2 that he is going to prepare a place for His followers, but again we are not told anything about its location, except that it is in Jesus' presence. In my church, the Missouri-Synod Lutheran Church, we believe that immediately upon death, our souls depart and are united with the Lord in paradise.

We do not believe though, that this is it, the way we will spend eternity. The Scriptures tell us that there is more and we believe that Jesus will return to the earth again. Jesus will restore what was cursed and make it new. On the day of the final judgment, the redeemed souls in heaven will be reunited with their own (now glorified) bodies and will begin to enjoy the bliss of heaven in both body and soul.

In John 5:28-29, Jesus says, "Do not be amazed at this, for a time is coming when all who are in their graves will hear his voice and come out--those who have done good will rise to live, and those who have done evil will rise to be condemned."

In 1 Corinthians 15, Paul goes into detail on how these bodies are as a seed and that they will rise into a new body that will dwell with the Lord on the new earth.

> There are also heavenly bodies, and there are earthly bodies, but the splendor of the heavenly bodies is one kind, and the splendor of the earthly bodies is another. The sun has one kind of splendor, the moon another and the stars another; and star differs from star in splendor. So will it be with the resurrection of the dead. The body that is sown is perishable; it is raised imperishable; it is sown in dishonor, it is raised in glory; it is sown in weakness, it is raised in power; it is sown a natural body, it is raised a spiritual body. If there is a natural body, there is also a spiritual body. (Chapter 15:40-44 NIV)

The Lutheran church has always rejected as unscriptural the idea that the soul "sleeps" between death and Judgment Day in such a way that it is not conscious of heavenly bliss.

Revelation 21 says,

Then I saw a new heaven and a new earth, for the first heaven and the first earth had passed away, and there was no longer any sea. I saw the Holy City, the New Jerusalem, coming down out of heaven from God, prepared as a bride beautifully dressed for her husband. And I heard a loud voice from the throne saying, "Now the dwelling of God is with men, and he will live with them. They will be his people, and God himself will be with them and be their God. He will wipe every tear from their eyes. There will be no more death or mourning or crying or pain, for the old order of things has passed away." He who was seated on the throne said, "I am making everything new!" Then he said, "Write this down, for these words are trustworthy and true." He said to me: "It is done. I am the Alpha and the Omega, the Beginning and the End. To him who is thirsty, I will give to drink without cost from the spring of the water of life. He who overcomes will inherit all this, and I will be his God, and he will be my son. But the cowardly, the unbelieving, the vile, the murderers, the sexually immoral, those who practice magic arts, the idolaters and all liars--their place will be in the fiery lake of burning sulfur. This is the second death. (1-8 NIV)

Isaiah 25:6-9, On this mountain, the LORD Almighty will prepare a feast of rich food for all peoples, a banquet of aged wine-- the best of meats and the finest of wines. On this mountain he will destroy the shroud that enfolds all peoples, the sheet that covers all nations; he will swallow up death forever. The Sovereign LORD will wipe away the tears from all faces; he will remove the disgrace of his people from all the earth. The LORD has spoken. In that day they will say, "Surely this is our God; we trusted in him, and he saved us. This is the LORD, we trusted in him; let us rejoice and be glad in his salvation." (NIV)

This is Eden restored. Remember in Genesis 3 after the fall of mankind; people were driven from the presence of the Lord? The most important thing for us to think about with heaven; is that it is living in the presence of the Lord. It is also important to see what God is doing here. People are not taken away to someplace out there or in the sky in safety, as the earth will be destroyed like a massive atomic bomb.

No, the earth will be made new, restored, redeemed by our Lord, even as his people are renewed and restored with a new, glorious and real body living with Him. That is heaven. We can say that for sure based on the Holy Scriptures. This is NOT a backup plan, something to be dreaded or feared. This is THE fulfillment of who we were created to be. It could not get any better than this.

It is difficult to say much more about heaven, other than it is dwelling with the Lord in Eden restored. Imagine living as Adam and Eve before the Fall, walking and working in the presence of the Creator, Living God. In many ways, it would seem that heaven is beyond our capacity to know and comprehend on this side of eternity. John offers a description of the New Jerusalem in Revelation 21:9-27, which almost seems as if he is saying it is so incredible and amazing that I cannot find enough words to describe it. The words match our theme in explaining the most essential thing of heaven and also its indescribable radiance and glory are due to the presence of the Lord:

Verse 21:11: It shone with the glory of God, and its brilliance was like that of a very precious jewel, like a jasper, clear as crystal.

21:22-23: I did not see a temple in the city because the Lord God Almighty and the Lamb are its temple. The city does not need the sun or the moon to shine on it, for the glory of God gives it light, and the Lamb is its lamp.

The presence of the Lord!

Indescribable! Incomprehensible! That is heaven. The Scriptures offer us more, but they do not give us everything. What they provide is enough; living in the presence of the Lord.

John 3:16, "For God so loved the world that he gave his one and only Son, that whoever believes in him shall not perish, but have eternal life." Life in the Presence of the Lord!

1 Corinthians 2:9, "However, as it is written: No eye has seen, no ear has heard, no mind has conceived what God

has prepared for those who love Him." It must be amazing!

PART THREE – DEPTH
I want to Know More
T.I.M.E. # 14

Here is a CHALLENGE for those who desire a deeper understanding of Christianity.

The following section is for those who want to know more about the Bible and the Christian faith. You will see topics and descriptions of the topic with the Biblical response. There are many references to particular Biblical passages corresponding to each topic. Feel free to look up as many as you desire. You do not have to look up any, as the descriptions are a paraphrase of what is written in the Bible, although reading the Bible while discovering for yourself is transformative. Approach this in a manner that works best for you. Use it as a means to grow in your relationship with Jesus as you gain a deeper understanding of the Christian Faith. This section could be considered the CliffNotes of the Bible and Christian Faith.

Scripture and Love (Faith 101)

Love is the central message of Scripture. I know, love is one of those words that makes men uncomfortable. But, I am not talking about that kind of love. 1 John 4:8 tells us that God is love. It would seem that love is the defining theme of the grand narrative of God's message given through the Bible. At the beginning in Genesis 1:26 God says let us create humankind in our image indicating that people were to be about love just as God is love. The remainder of God's message, which is the entire Scripture, tells the story of God's love for humankind. The great rescue operation is worked out, beginning with the Lord God showing grace to the first humans by clothing them and sending them away sparing their lives, which were no longer able to dwell in His presence after the first sins were committed. Jesus states in Matthew 5:17-18 that he has come to fulfill what the prophets and the law teach. When asked which part of the law is the most critical Jesus told us in Matthew 22:37-40 that we are to love God above all things and that we are to love our neighbor as ourselves. Further, Jesus said that all of the law hung on these two commandments. The central message of Scripture is one of restoring proper love in creation.

You shall love the Lord your God with all your heart, and with all your soul, and with all your mind.

God told Abram "I am God Almighty, walk before me, and be blameless" (Genesis 17:1). Psalm 33:8 says, "Let all the earth fear the Lord; let all the people of the world revere Him." Scripture is filled with examples of God commanding people to love Him and put him first (Deuteronomy 6:5, Psalm 33:8, Psalm 73:25-26, Psalm 96:4, Psalm 11:10, Proverbs 3:5, Matthew 4:10, Matthew 10:28, Matthew 10:37, and Matthew 22:37 to name a few). It becomes clear in the Biblical narrative that we were created to love and serve the one and only God who created us for that purpose.

Love your neighbor as yourself

A natural result of loving God above all else is obeying His commands. Jesus said that if we love Him we will obey and we do this by following his command to love each other as he has loved us. 1 John 4:12 tells us if we love one another God lives in us and His love is perfected in us. Again Matthew 7:12 states, "In everything, do to others what you would have them do to you, for this sums up the Law and the Prophets." Our marching orders as followers of Jesus are to spread the love of God that resides in us (Mark 12:33, Luke 6:27, John 13:34, John 15:17, Romans 13:9, 1 Corinthians 16:14, Galatians 5:14, Ephesians 4:2, Philippians 1:9, Colossians 1:4, Hebrews 13:1, and 1John 4:7 only scratch the surface of passages).

Love is the central message of the entire Scripture. There is just no way for an atheistic worldview to explain the presence of love in our world. There is absolutely no way for love to have naturally developed through millions of millions of years of evolution, or any other worldview for that matter. God created love. God is love. Jesus is God who walked among us and demonstrated His love by dying to restore His Creation. Jesus describes Himself as the fulfillment of the Scriptures (Matthew 26:56, Luke 24:44-45). 1 John 3:11 tells us that the message heard from the beginning is about love and this love is further described in 1 John 4:7-21. Jesus confirms this through the words He spoke (John 13:34-35), but most importantly through His life and ultimate sacrifice on the cross. It is all about love! Now some may not think of "love" as a manly thing. But, love in the way described in Scripture, the love demonstrated by the Lord God and His Son Jesus is the manliest verb we possess in our language. Let's look at this love as we seek to know who God is.

Scripture and Love

Scripture, or what many call the Holy Bible, is the story of God in history. It is the narrative of a Creator who is love itself (1 John 4:8). The story begins in Genesis as all things are created with humans being the pinnacle of this divine act created in the image of God, who were to be the caretakers of it all. The freedom granted by the Lord God involved a choice to live freely in this perfect fellowship with God and the created order versus becoming like God knowing good and evil through eating from the tree forbidden by God (Genesis 3). Following the Genesis account of people choosing to break perfect fellowship with God, the entire Scripture records the story of the Lord God working to restore His perfect created order. Jesus described himself as the fulfillment of the Scriptures (Matthew 26:54-56) and interpreted all that is written in them in relation to himself (Luke 24:24 ff). Scripture reveals God's motive for all of this in John 3:16 as being an act of love. Many know this verse by heart: "For God so loved the world that he gave his only Son, so that everyone who believes in him may not perish but may have eternal life." The New Testament shows that followers of Jesus become empowered to participate in God's action of restoration (John 14:15-17, 23, 26, 15:5, 10-17, 17:15-25, Acts 2:38, 1 John 4:11-13, to name a few). Thus, Scripture reveals a grand narrative, which has been ongoing throughout time; further, we are all participants in this story. This very Scripture describes itself as being revealed by the Holy Spirit of God (2 Timothy 3:16, 2 Peter 1:19-21). Jesus testified that the OT and his teachings were the word of God (Matthew 25:35, 5:17-18, John 14:10 & 24).

In this next section, you will find short descriptions of aspects of this God of love. These are written to give brief Biblical responses and references to some of the "churchy" words you may have heard but are nonetheless beliefs Christians hold. The Scripture references are listed for you to look up either as you read or to reference later.

The God of Love

The attributes of God

1 John 4:12 says that no one has ever seen God, however, if we love we can know God through His Spirit dwelling in us. While we know that God is a God of love and that this is to be His followers' mission, Romans 11:33 reminds us that God is beyond our ability to know truly and understand (Job 26:14, Psalm 145:3, Isaiah 55:8-9). God is described as perfect (Matthew 5:38, Psalm 18:30), omniscient (Job 37:16, Psalm 139:1-4, Isaiah 46:9-10, Hebrews 4:13, 1 John 4:12), almighty (Genesis 35:11, Job 11:7, Revelation 19:6), holy (1 Samuel 2:2, Isaiah 6:3, Hosea 11:9, John 17:11), sovereign (Psalm 8:1,9, Isaiah 1:24, Acts 4:24, 1 Timothy 6:15), faithful (Deuteronomy 7:9, 32:4, Psalm 31:5, 1 Corinthians 1:9, 10:13, 2 Corinthians 1:18, 1 Timothy 5:24), righteous (Psalm 7:11, 11:7, Isaiah 24:16, Romans 2:5, 1 John 2:1) and gracious (Exodus 34:6, 2 Chronicles 30:9, Nehemiah 9:31, Psalm 86:15, 116:5) to name but a few. The book of Job outlines humans' inability to fully comprehend and understand God as experienced by Job. Our finite, human nature places God beyond our ability to describe appropriately, and yet

we find comfort from Psalm 8:4 knowing that this God is mindful of us.

The Trinity

You may have heard the term and been confused or had a difficult time grasping its meaning. The Holy Trinity is a core doctrine of Protestantism stating that there is one true God, one Divine essence, while at the same time there are three distinct persons, the Father, the Son, and the Holy Spirit (Matthew 28:19, 2 Corinthians 13:13). Although the term Trinity never appears in the Scriptures, the activity of God presents itself in a "Trinitarian" manner; we see God working as a trinity (John 14:16, 26, 16:13-15, 20:21-22, 1 Corinthians 12:4-6, 2 Corinthians 1:21-22, Galatians 4:6, Ephesians 2:20-22). This same action is found in the Old Testament (Psalm 119:89, Proverbs 1:20-23, Ezekiel 36:26). The Father, Son, and Holy Spirit are all presented as being fully God (Father: Genesis 1, John 17, Galatians 1; Son: John 1, Hebrews 1, Revelation 1; Holy Spirit: Ezekiel 37, John 3, I Peter 1:2).

The works of the God of Love
Creation

The Scriptures tell us that God created the heavens and the earth and everything in them (Genesis 1 and 2, Job 38:44-7, Psalm 33:6) by his word. Not only is God the source of everything that is, but also the sustainer (Nehemiah 9:6). God did not create due to unmet needs or inadequacies (Acts 17:24-25); God's creation brings delight and glory (Isaiah 43:7, 62:3-5, Zephaniah 3:17, Ephesians 1:11-12). The Scriptures describe creation as an outpouring of God's love (Psalm 19:1, Psalm 33:5-6, John 1:1-5 Ephesians 1:4-5).

Providence

God not only created, but He is also intimately involved in loving and sustaining all that was created (Psalm 103:17-18, Psalm 136, Hebrews 1:3). The Lord provides for our every need (Psalm 104), and it is in Him we have our very being (Acts 17:28). God works everything out according to the purpose of his will (Ephesians 1:11). Without the providence of God creation would cease (Nehemiah 9:6, Colossians 1:17, Hebrews 1:3).

Angels and demons; Satan

The Scriptures record much activity regarding angels or messengers (Matthew 1, Luke 1, Luke 24). Angels are reported as attendants and ministers (Psalm 91:11-12, Daniel 7:10, Hebrews 1:14). There is also the presence of demons that seek to destroy the good (Mark 5:9, Ephesians 6:12, Mark 4:15, 1 Peter 5:8-9). Examples of Satan's motives and actions are included in the narratives of the temptation of Eve and Adam (Genesis 3), seeking to destroy Job (Job 2), and in the temptation of Jesus (Matthew 4:1-11).

Love expressed/Humanity
The makeup of human nature

God said, "Let us make humankind in our image, according to our likeness" (Genesis 1:26), forming man from the dust of the ground and breathing the breath of life into his nostrils (Genesis 2:7). God continues to create. Psalm 139:13 says "For it was you who formed my inward parts; you knit me together in my mother's womb." Humans are created with physical (body) and non-physical natures (soul/spirit) (Luke 1:46-47, 1 Thessalonians 5:23, Hebrews 4:12), which are connected. Man and woman are both created in God's image (Genesis 1:27) being more like God than anything in creation. Men and women are created with distinct roles, which are to be equal and harmonious (Genesis 2:18, 1 Corinthians 11:8-10, 1 Timothy 2:13). Even though the first humans were created in the image of God, it seems that after "the Fall" people were created in the image of their fathers (Genesis 5:3). This is the reason all people are born sinful and unclean. Our relationship with God was broken (Romans 3:23). The likeness of God is restored through Jesus when the spirit is renewed (Ephesians 4:24).

The purpose of humanity

After God created humankind in his image Scripture says that God blessed them and sent out to be fruitful, fill the earth and subdue it (Genesis 1:28). As beings created by almighty God they should have loved him above all things (Revelation 4:11), they were to spread and share the blessings of God and ultimately do everything to glorify God (Genesis 1:28, 1 Corinthians 10:31). In working out God's plan of restoration after he was resurrected, before his ascension, Jesus told his disciples that he was sending them out to all nations proclaiming God's love received by faith through the Holy Spirit (Luke 24:45-48). In Matthew's account, Jesus tells the disciples that they are being sent to make disciples by baptizing in the name of the Father, Son, and Holy Spirit teaching them to observe all that Jesus had commanded them (Matthew 28:19-20). Earlier in Matthew Jesus had been questioned as to what were the greatest commandments, whereby Jesus answered to love the Lord with all your heart and strength and to also love your neighbor as yourself. He further stated that on these two commandments hung all of the law (Matthew 22:35-40, Mark 12:28-31). John 15:12 also includes Jesus' command to love each other as he has loved; furthermore, Jesus includes all believers in his commissioning as he mentions us as those who will believe in him through the disciple's testimony in John 17:20-21. Our purpose is to love as God loves.

Love of self/Sin
The nature of sin

Sin came into the world through the first humans (Genesis 3:1-7, Psalm 51:5, Romans 5:19) and as a result people are unable to live holy lives in fellowship with God or others (Psalm 51:5, Romans 5:12). All sin is idolatry, or an attempt to put something in place of God, originating in our desire to "be like God." Since all people are the offspring of the first humans we are born into sin, therefore our deeds are evil (Galatians 5:19-21, 1 John 1:8-10). The book of Romans states that all people are under the power of sin; it is a part of human nature (Romans 3:9-23, 7:18). The very core of sin is in our hearts (Isaiah 29:13, Jeremiah 5:23, 17:9-10, Ezekiel 36:26, Matthew 15:19). The result is that we are unable to follow God's command to love the Lord our God with all our heart, soul and might (Deuteronomy 6:5, Matthew 22:37, Mark 12:30). Under the power of sin, our desires are controlled by the world (1 John 2:15-17).

The effects of sin

The apostle Paul describes the effects of sin through an explanation of the inner conflict within himself as he is unable to do the good he knows he should since sin dwells in him (Romans 5:19, 7:15-20). This is the result of the first sin, which came into the world through the first humans (Romans 5:12). All people are incapable of good and right actions (Psalm 14:1-3, Isaiah 64:6, John 8:34, Romans 3:10-12, Hebrews 11:6). God tells Moses in

Exodus that no one can see God and live (Exodus 33:20). Ultimately, we are no longer able to live in fellowship with God, as did Adam and Eve before the first sins when they seemingly had face-to-face conversations with him (Genesis 2-3). Furthermore, everyone will experience death (Genesis 2:17).

The punishment for sin

God is a just God, therefore must punish people
for their sins (Jeremiah 9:24). God cannot tolerate sin and wicked people (Isaiah 5:25, Hosea 8:5, Zechariah 10:3). Scripture is full of references to a time when God will judge the people (Psalm 7:8, Ecclesiastes 3:17, Hebrews 10:30, 1 Peter 2:12 to name a few). Jesus describes a time when cities will be judged, and those who do not repent will be brought down to Hades (Matthew 11:20-24). In Luke 16:19-31 Jesus tells the story of Lazarus and the rich man who neglected him daily. After they both had died, angels carried Lazarus to be with Abraham while the rich man was sent to Hades a place of burning and torment. To prevent his brothers from also entering Hades, Lazarus asks Abraham to send someone from the dead to warn his brothers. Abraham states that they will not repent even if

someone rises from the dead and goes to them. And while all people are born into this condition unable to repent or accept the things of God, we have hope knowing that through love Jesus was sent by God to restore his creation (Romans 6:23, 8:37).

Jesus Christ/Love in action
The humanity of Jesus Christ

The Scriptures present Jesus as being fully
human and fully divine; this is a somewhat difficult concept to understand, yet Jesus' followers accept it through faith. The Scriptures are clear in presenting Jesus as fully human (1 Timothy 2:5, Luke 24:39, Matthew 4:2, John 19:28). It was necessary for this true man to live under the law to fulfill the law to rescue all those who are born into the condition of sin (Galatians 4:4-5, Romans 5:19, Colossians 1:22, Hebrews 2:14). This priest has lived the perfect life as a human to redeem his followers (Hebrews 4:14-16). John 15:13 tells us that Jesus performed this amazing action out of love.

The deity of Jesus Christ

It was necessary for Jesus also to be fully God because no one born after the first sins (Genesis 3) are capable of living the perfect life, thereby fulfilling the law (Psalm 49:7, Galatians 4:4-5, 1 Peter 1:18-19). As one who is fully God (Matthew 17:5, John 1:17-18), Jesus was without sin (Luke 2:40, John 8:46, Acts 2:27, 2 Corinthians 5:21, 1 Peter 4:15). As such, Jesus has reconciled his followers to God and is the mediator between God and people (Colossians 1:19-20, 1 Timothy 2:5, Hebrews 2:17). He was given the authority to perform this incredible act of love on our behalf (John 10:11-18).

The Atonement

Isaiah 53: 4-5 expresses God's plan of redemption. God loves his creation and indeed intends to rescue it (John 3:16-17). God desires for his people to be free and to live as they were created to live (John 8:34-36, Hebrews 2:14-17, 1 Peter 2:24). Jesus took away the sins of the world (John 1:29, 1 John 2:2), to set people free from the bondage of sin (John 8:34-36), so that people can love the Lord God with their entire heart, soul, and might (Philippians 2:9-11). Jesus is the fulfillment of this rescue operation and the one who stands in our place before God (1 Timothy 2:3-6). Ultimately, Jesus died and paid the price for our sins (1 Corinthians 15:3), which is obtained through repentance and faith in Him (Mark 1:15). Jesus' resurrection establishes Jesus as king of the world inaugurating a new kingdom and a new covenant with His people (1 Corinthians 15:20-28). Just as atonement performed by the priests served in God dwelling among his people Israel under the old covenant; Jesus' atoning sacrifice provides the offering, which allows God to dwell among us under the New Covenant (Jeremiah 33:14-16).

The Holy Spirit/Love empowered from on High

The Holy Spirit is the third person of the Trinity.

The Scriptures present the Holy Spirit as distinct from the Father and the Son (Matthew 28:19, John 14:26, Galatians 4:6). The Holy Spirit is God, which is demonstrated through the attributes the Spirit possesses (Psalm 139:7-10, Hebrews 9:14, Titus 3:5, 1 Peter 4:14).

Work of the Spirit

The Holy Spirit sanctifies followers of Jesus (1

Corinthians 6:11, Titus 3:5) and allows them to accept the things of God (Romans 8:7, 1 Corinthians 2:14, 1 Corinthians 12:3). This is accomplished through grace, which is God's undeserved love (Ephesians 2:8-9) by the power of the Holy Spirit given to us (Romans 15:13). Joel 2, Jeremiah 31 and Ezekiel 39 describe the prophecy given by God that declares the outpouring of the Holy Spirit and the manner in which the Spirit will bring understanding and open the way to fellowship with God (Acts 2). This is the "power from on high" that Jesus spoke of in Luke 24:49. Clothed with the Holy Spirit, we become a new creation (2 Corinthians 5:17, 1 Peter 1:23) empowered to do good works (Ephesians 2:10) and to obey what Jesus commanded (John 14:15, 15:5).

Gifts of the Spirit

Paul tells the Christians of the Church in Corinth
(1 Corinthians 1:2) they are God's temple and that God's Spirit dwells within them (1Corinthians 3:16). Ephesians 2:20-22 echoes the Corinthian passage telling the people that they are being joined together to become a dwelling in which God lives by His Spirit. This Spirit that dwells within gives gifts that are to be used in service to others

for the common good (1 Corinthians 12:7). Fundamentally, Paul tells the Corinthian church that their gifts are to be used to love others (1 Corinthians 13:1-3). If we are living by the Spirit, the results will be love, joy, peace, patience, kindness, generosity, faithfulness, gentleness and self-control (Galatians 5:22-23). All of this is to build up the Body of Christ, spreading the faith and knowledge of Jesus as His followers build on the foundation of love (Ephesians 4:12-16). This is the working out of Jesus' words (John 13:34-35, John 14:15-23).

Salvation/Rescued in Love
Union with Christ

In John 15:1-17 Jesus speaks of the importance of remaining in Him and that those who abide in Him will bear much fruit, which is following Jesus' command to love one another (John 15:17). John described union with Christ being present if we believe in Jesus Christ and love one another (1 John 3:23-24). It is this revelation of God's love that we can live in Christ and Christ in us (1 John 4:9-13).

Grace

Grace comes to us through Jesus (John 1:17, Romans 5:15, 1 Corinthians 1:4). In Ephesians Paul states that it is by grace you have been saved through faith, not of your own doing, it is the gift of God (Ephesians 2:8). Grace as the love of God is seen throughout the narrative of Scripture occurring immediately in Genesis 3:21 when the Lord God clothed Adam and Eve sparring their lives after the first sins. Jesus, as the fulfillment of the law, (Matthew 26:56, Luke 24:44-45, Galatians 4:4-6) life, and mission was an act of the Grace of God.

Faith/Repentance

After Peter's speech at Pentecost in Acts chapter two, where he spoke of Jesus' life and role as the Messiah, the people who heard were convicted and wanted their sins forgiven and to be saved. Peter told them that they should repent of their sins, which is asking God for forgiveness and being baptized in the name of Jesus Christ (Acts 2:37-38). People's reconciliation with God comes both through faith in Jesus (Acts 10:43, Romans 10:17) and repentance (Acts 11:15-18).

Regeneration

The ability to respond to God in faith is given after "rebirth, renewal, or regeneration" in the Spirit (John 3:3-5, Titus 3:5-8). Peter states that we are to love one another earnestly since we have been reborn (1 Peter 1:22-23). Jesus told Nicodemus that people must be born again to enter the kingdom of heaven and then went on to say that this is accomplished through believing in Him because God sent Him into the world to save it. God so loved the world (John 3).

Justification

Paul said "For there is no distinction; for all have sinned and fall short of the glory of God, and are justified by his grace as a gift, through the redemption that is in Christ Jesus" (Romans 3:23-24). Further, "For we hold that one is justified by faith apart from works of the law" (Romans 3:28). This justification comes after the "new birth" that Jesus speaks of in John 3. We are made-right through believing in our Lord Jesus (John 3:16-17, Acts 10:43).

227

Sanctification

Sanctification is a "building up" or maturation
where the believer enters a process becoming holy or more
like Jesus through life in Him (Acts 20:32). Sanctification
is a result of freedom to live in God (Romans 6:22). The
result of abiding in this love is that we are free to love God
and others as we grow in holiness (1 Peter 1:15-16, 1 John
4:18).

Glorification

Glorification will occur when Jesus comes again,
and the believers will receive His glory and those who
were justified will be glorified (Romans 8:28-30, 1
Corinthians 15, Hebrews 9:27-28).

The Church/Love for the world
Nature, Mission, and Function of the Church

The church is the bride of Christ (Ephesians 5:25-27), and
Jesus is the head of this "body" (Colossians 1:18) and it is
comprised of those who place their faith in Jesus Christ (1

Corinthians 1:2). All believers are considered members of the church joining in worship and service becoming more and more like Christ (1 Peter 2:5). The church is compared to a body with each member performing a role in its healthy function (Romans 12:4-5, Ephesians 4:4-16). Followers of Jesus, who are this church, are commanded to go into the world sharing the love of God (Matthew 28:19-20, John 20:21, Acts 1:8, 1 Peter 2:9). Acts 2:42-47 further describes the manner in which, believers conducted themselves when they met together in love as expressed by Jesus through the apostles. As members of this church (John 15) we are to live as we share God's message of love (John 3:16) through a life of action expressed through loving others through truth and action (1 John 3:16-24).

Offices of the Church

Paul says that the church is the body of Christ and that God has appointed some members to be "apostles, second prophets, third teachers, then miracles, then gifts of healing, helping, administrating and various kinds of tongues" (1 Corinthians 12:28), "the apostles, the prophets, the evangelists, the shepherds, and the teachers" (Ephesians 4:11). Following these listings, Paul says similar words to those of Jesus and John stating that it is truly all about love, which is even greater than faith and hope (1 Corinthians 13 and Ephesians 4:16).

Sacraments of the Church

The sacraments practiced by Protestant churches today are baptism and the Lord's Supper/Holy Communion (Acts 2:38, Luke 22:19).

Baptism

Jesus sent his disciples into the world to make disciples stating that they were to baptize them in the name of the Father, Son, and Holy Spirit, teaching them to obey everything that He commanded (Matthew 28:19-20). Peter demonstrated this command in Acts 2 when asked what must be done in response to the message of Jesus that he had delivered: "Repent, and be baptized every one of you in the name of Jesus Christ so that your sins may be forgiven; and you will receive the gift of the Holy Spirit" (Acts 2:38). Mark tells us that whoever believes and is baptized will be saved (Mark 16:16). Paul tells us that those who were baptized into Christ were baptized into his death and that this will result in union with Him in His resurrection (Romans 6:3-5) and in Galatians, he tells us that baptism clothes us in Christ (Galatians 3:27).

The Lord's Supper, Holy Communion

Jesus instituted the Lord's Supper on the night he was betrayed telling the disciples to "take and eat, this is my body...this is my blood (Matthew 26:26-28) telling them to do this in remembrance of Him (Luke 22:19). Jesus said that the cup was the "new covenant in my blood" (Luke 22:20), which is poured out for many for the forgiveness of sins (Matthew 26:28). Hebrews states Jesus is the mediator of a new covenant inaugurated through his blood and death, describing Jesus as the high priest of the good things that have come (Hebrews 9:11-22). The good things are putting God's laws in their hearts, and writing them on their minds; remembering their sins and lawless deeds no more (Jeremiah 31:33-34 as cited in Hebrews 10:16-17). When we participate in the Lord's Supper, we are receiving and proclaiming His sacrifice for the forgiveness of sins, which is also ours (1 Corinthians 11:26).

The Last Things/Love fulfilled Death

Hebrews 9:27 states that "it is appointed for mortals to die once and after that face the judgment." Romans 8:10 tells us that our body is dead because of sin, which was the direct result of turning away from the Lord God's ways and commands (Genesis 2:15-17, Ezekiel 18:4). Since all people are born into sin, everyone must die (Psalm 51:5, Romans 3:23, 5:12). Revelation tells us of the good news 'the last things/love fulfilled,' "and from Jesus Christ, the faithful witness, the firstborn of the dead, and the ruler of the kings of the earth. To him who loves us and freed us from our sins by his blood, and made us to be a kingdom, priests serving his God and Father, to him be glory and dominion forever and ever. Amen" (Revelation 1:5-6). All believers will share in this eternal life of which, Jesus is the firstborn (John 11:25-26, John 14:19, 1 Corinthians 15:20). There is evidence in the Scriptures that upon death, believers join Jesus until the time of His second coming (Luke 23:43, Acts 7:59, Philippians 1:23-24, Revelation 19:13).

Second coming

The last things will occur when Jesus' return to earth. Jesus will come surrounded by his angels (Matthew 16:27, 2 Thessalonians 1:7, Jude 14) and a resurrection of the dead will take place, and Jesus will judge both the living and the dead. The followers of Jesus will receive salvation, and those who did not follow Jesus will be condemned (Daniel 12:1-2, Matthew 25:31-46, John 5:27-29, 6:39-54, Acts 10:42, 1 Corinthians 15:12-57, Revelation 20:11-15). Jesus will destroy death and Satan (1 Corinthians 15:26-57), 2 Thessalonians 2:8, Revelation 12:10-11, 20-14). When Jesus returns a new heaven and earth will be created (2 Peter 3:10-13 Revelation 21:1-2).

The Resurrection

Jesus' death and resurrection defeated sin, death and Satan (Mark 8:31, Romans 6:9, Hebrews 2:14). Jesus said that those who believe in him will share in the resurrection (John 11:25-26). Further, those who receive salvation from Jesus will be raised with a new body to spend eternity with Him (Job 19:25-27, John 5:28-29, 1 Corinthians 15:20-57, 1 Thessalonians 4:16). The holy city, the New Jerusalem will come down from heaven, and God will make His home among the people (Revelation 21:2-3). "Then he said to me, 'It is done! I am the Alpha and Omega, the beginning and the end. To the thirsty, I will give water as a gift from the spring of the water of life. Those who conquer will inherit these things, and I will be their God, and they will be my children'" (Revelation 6-7). We place our hope in these promises knowing that we are already God's children who will one day be completely conformed to Christ's image (1 John 3:2) and will put on immortality (1 Corinthians 15:53-54). 1 Corinthians 15:49 states that before death we have the image of the man of dust, but will also bear the image of Jesus (Romans 8:29, Colossians 3:10). The Scriptures tell this story of love, which is still being fulfilled until Jesus returns with the New Jerusalem when the Lord God will again dwell among the people and be their God (Revelation 21).

The End Times

The Scriptures seem to be somewhat ambiguous regarding entrance into heaven and hell. Jesus told the criminal executed beside him that today he would be with him in paradise (Luke 23:43) and Paul states that he desires to depart and be with the Lord (Philippians 1:23), which both indicate an immediate joining Jesus upon death. Jesus' story in Luke 16:19-31 describes a sense of a world with God and one separated from Him; however, the force of the story appears to be addressing the danger of riches and selfish living upon the earth. Jesus' teaching is perhaps more directed towards the manner in which one is to live upon this earth since he has risen from the dead and established the new covenant; there is not a great deal written about a future time in heaven.

The Scriptures identify a time of judgment, the second coming of Jesus (Matthew 24:29-30, 25:31, 2 Timothy 4:1, 2 Thessalonians 2:8, Hebrews 9:26-28) where the dead or those who sleep in the earth will be judged according to the manner in which they lived (Daniel 12:2, Matthew 16:27, John 5:25-29, Hebrews 9:27). The time of this judgment is unknown (Matthew 24:42, 25:13, Mark 13:32, 37, Acts 1:7). The righteous will receive eternal life while those who did not minister as Jesus did will receive eternal punishment (Matthew 25:31-46, Revelation 21:7-8).

Finally, the new heavens and a new earth will be

established, and God will dwell among His people (2 Peter 3:1-13, Revelation 21-22).

This overview, or brief look at the Christian faith and who God is forms the foundation of our beliefs. Remember, our beliefs inform and shape all of our actions. That is the beginning of understanding who you are and why you are here. It is the beginning of living a life as **one who has found** what they were looking for.

But these are written so that you may come to believe that Jesus is the Messiah, the Son of God, and that through believing you may have life in his name.
John 20:31

About the author

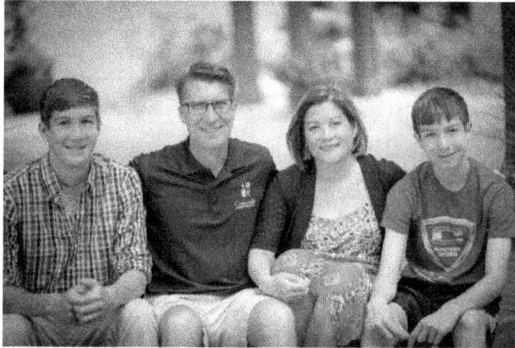

Francis Green is a pastor in the Lutheran Church-Missouri Synod serving in Minnesota.

He spent more than ten years skydiving with over 2000 jumps, over 30 hours of freefall time, with tandem master, jumpmaster, instructor and parachute rigger ratings. Fran served on the Air Force Parachute Team, The Wings of Blue from 1988-1992.

Fran and Tammy have two sons, Zeke and Silas.

But my life is worth nothing to me unless I use it for finishing the work assigned me by the Lord Jesus – the work of telling others the Good News about the wonderful grace of God. Acts 20:24

Notes

1 Strong Enterprises. (1996, July 2). Strong's Report on Ron Green/M. Colby Tandem. Retrieved March 15, 2017, from https://groups.google.com/forum/#!topic/rec.skydivin g/lGaia8ajiFw

2 Elmore, T. Growing Leaders. (2014, July 16). One Antidote to Male Disillusionment [Blog post]. Retrieved March 15, 2017, from https://growingleaders.com/blog/one-antidote-to-male- disillusionment/

3 Radcliff, B. (2015). "An Epidemic of Hopelessness?" Retrieved November 2, 2017, from https://psychologytoday.com/blog/the-economy-happiness/201511/epidemic-hopelessness

4 Dawkins, R. (2006). *The God Delusion*. New York, NY: Houghton Mifflin.

5 DiCarlo, C. (2011). *How to Become a Really Good Pain in the Ass: A Critical Thinker's Guide to Asking the the Right Questions*. Amherst, NY: Prometheus Books.

6 Lennox, J. (2015). *Against the Flow, The*

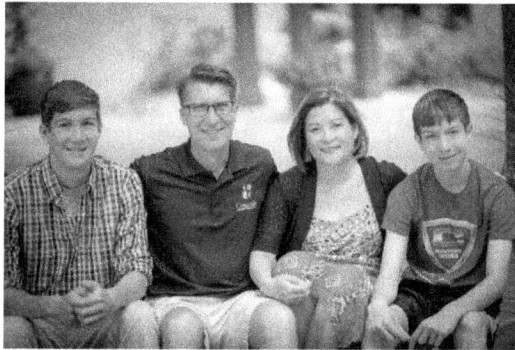

Inspiration of Daniel in an Age of Relativism.
Oxford, England: Monarch Books.

Eagleton, T. London Review of Books. (2006,
October 19). Lunging, Flailing, Mispunching.
Retrieved March 15, 2017, from
https://www.lrb.co.uk/v28/n20/terry-
eagleton/lunging-flailing- mispunching

8 Tacitus, Annals 15.44, cited in Strobel, The Case for
Christ, 82.

9 Pliny, Letters, transl. by William Melmoth, rev. by
W.M.L. Hutchinson (Cambridge: Harvard Univ.
Press, 1935), vol. II, X:96, cited in Habermas, The
Historical Jesus, 199.

10 Lewis, C.S., *Mere Christianity.* London: Collins,
1952, pp. 54–56. (In all editions, this is Bk. II, Ch. 3,
"The Shocking Alternative.")

11 Wolfmueller, B. (2016). *Has American
Christianity Failed?* St. Louis, MO: Concordia
Publishing House.

12 As cited in, Campolo, T. (2000). *Let Me Tell You a
Story.* Nashville, TN: W. Publishing Group.

[13] Kinnaman, D. & Lyons, G. (2016). *Good Faith, Being a Christian When Society Thinks You're Irrelevant and Extreme*. Grand Rapids, MI: Baker Books.

[14] Ibid.

[15] O'Reilly, D. "A Study Asks: What's a Church's Economic Worth?" *Philadelphia Inquirer,* February 1, 2011, http://articles.philly.com/2011-02-01/news/27092987_1_partners-for-sacred-places-congregations-churches.

[16] Berlinski, D. (2009). *The Devil's Delusion Atheism and Its Scientific Pretensions.* New York, NY: Basic Books.